DENMARK
IN PRINT AND
PICTURES

THE
DANISH CHURCH

Editor

Poul Hartling

DET DANSKE SELSKAB

*The Danish Institute for Information about Denmark and
Cultural Cooperation with Other Nations*

Through the porch we enter the church (*vide* page 2). Rind Church, County of Ringkøbing.

Preceding pages :

1. It is the ambition of the parish that the whitewashed walls of its church shine across the landscape like a beacon. Our picture shows Hansted Church (near Horsens in Jutland) being whitewashed.

2. (the double page). Vester Skerninge Church, in the island of Funen, dating from the 15th century, presents the typical Gothic exterior.

The hymns are sung while the congregation is seated (*vide* page 2).

On Sunday mornings the church bells ring . . . (*vide* page 1)

On Sunday mornings the church bells ring. In every parish in town and country the ringing tells us that the divine service is about to begin.

And they ring on weekdays, too. In the morning they ring at sunrise and the evening bell "rings the sun down". But on Sundays their ringing calls us to worship. Three times the bell is rung, the third time, five minutes before the church service begins, ends with three times three "prayer strokes".

There have been churches in Denmark for a thousand years. A traveller touring the country cannot but note the Danish village church, which, in many places, adds a characteristic touch to the landscape. With its church tower and corbie-stepped gables it is a unique piece of Danish architecture, a type of church that is hardly to be found anywhere else in the world. In the country towns we find the church in the market-place or in some other open square. In the larger towns it is often on the main street, built into the line of houses.

So the church is part of the Danish landscape, and of the town-scape, too, just as, by its work and history, the Church is part of Denmark. It has contributed to the evolution of our culture and view of life, its threads are woven into our literature and art.

This is a book about the Danish Church. It is to tell the reader about the life and work of the Church, its organization, buildings, and history. In this book an attempt will be made to answer the questions that may occur to any one trying to find out what the Danish Church is like.

The best way of becoming acquainted with the Church, is to enter it. Suppose, therefore, that one Sunday we accept the invitation of the church bell and enter. Everyone is welcome to do so.

Through an entrance hall (called the *arms-house,* because in olden times men would deposit their weapons there) we enter the church. It is an Evangelical-Lutheran nave with an altar, pulpit, and baptismal font. When the bells have ceased ringing, the service begins.

THE CHURCH SERVICE

After the last stroke of the bell, the service begins with the organ prelude. While it is being played, the priest enters and faces the altar.

The Entrance Prayer is read by a layman, the parish-clerk (or "church singer") as a representative of the congregation. This prayer dates from the 16th century, and became a permanent part of the service in 1685. (See page 54). It reads as follows:

Let us all pray: O Lord, I have come into this Thine house to hear what Thou, God the Father, my Creator, Thou Lord Jesus, my Saviour, Thou, Good Holy Ghost, in life and death my Comforter, wilt speak unto me. Lord, open now my heart by Thy Holy Ghost, for the sake of Jesus Christ, so that I may learn from Thy Word to repent of my sins, and in life and death to believe in Jesus, and day by day to improve in a holy life. May God hear and grant this through Jesus Christ. Amen.

Then follows *The First Hymn.* In Denmark the hymns are usually sung while the congregation is seated. Usually all the stanzas of the hymns are sung.

Salutation and Collect. After the hymn the priest faces the congregation, and says or chants: The Lord be with you! The congregation answers: and with thy spirit! The priest says: Let us all pray! turns to the altar, and reads the day's collect. For each Sunday and holiday there there is a special collect (common prayer). Most of the collects date from the time of the Reformation. The congregation sings: Amen.

The Epistle: Facing the congregation the priest says: The epistle writes the apostle . . . (or: This holy lesson is written in . . .), whereupon he reads the section of the epistle (or the lesson) that is appointed for the holiday in question. The congregation is standing while the Bible Text is being read. From olden times a special epistle-text (lesson) and a Gospel-text have been appointed for each Sunday and holiday. In 1895 a new series of texts (called the Second Series of Texts) was introduced, and now the two series alternate, the First Series being used in "odd" years, the Second Series in "even" years.

The Second Hymn is sung after the reading of the epistle.

The Gospel and the Creed. Facing the congregation, the priest says: *This holy Gospel is written by the Evangelist N. . . .* To which the congregation answers:

God be praised for these joyful tidings! and rises. The priest now reads the Gospel text of the series that is not in use that year. After the reading it is the custom in many churches to speak or sing the Renouncement and the Creed. While the creed is being spoken, the congregation stands. The congregation sings: *Amen,* and after that often a stanza of a hymn, *e.g.:*

> *Let not the world lead us astray,*
> *From our Baptismal Pact away,*
> *But grant that all our longings be,*
> *O, Lord, forever unto Thee!*
>
> (The Danish Hymnal No. 99, stanza 6).

The Third Hymn precedes the sermon. While it is being sung, the priest leaves the altar and enters the pulpit.

The Sermon. After a short extempore prayer the priest reads (the congregation rises) that Sunday's Gospel text, on which he is to preach.

The sermon ends with *Amen* and doxology:

Praise, thanks, and glory be to Thee our God, Father, Son and Holy Ghost, Thou who wast, and art, and shall be, one true Triune God, highly praised from the first beginning, now, and in all Eternity. Amen!

The Church Prayer. Here the priest can improvise or say the appointed prayer, which reads as follows:

Comfort and succour Thou, our God, all who are in sickness and sorrow, whether they be far or near. Let Thy gracious help be with all who suffer anguish, and stand by us all in the hour of temptation!

Bless and keep Thy Holy Universal Church, and us within it! Bless and keep Thy Holy Sacraments and let Thy Word have free course amongst us, that Thy Kingdom with righteousness and peace and joy in the Holy Ghost may increase and grow, and that the light of grace may shine before them that sit in darkness and in the shadow of death.

Stretch forth Thy protecting hand over our people and over our country and all its lawful authorities, bless and keep our King and Queen and the Royal House. Grant unto them and unto us all Thy grace, peace and blessing and, after a Christian life, eternal joy.

Our Father . . .

Announcements. Next follow the announcements of marriages, other announcements, and information is given of services and meetings in the near future, and perhaps of the "collect" (i. e. collection) which will be taken up. On special occasions, the congregation may bring their altar-offerings to the altar, but usually offerings are put into offertory boxes at the exit.

The Blessing. The priest pronounces the Blessing from the pulpit. Sometimes the "Aaronitic" (*vide infra*), but usually the "Apostolic" Blessing: *The grace of the Lord Jesus Christ, and the love of God, and the communion of the Holy Ghost be with us all. Amen.* (2. Cor. 13. 13). Sometimes there follows a motet, a chorus, or a stanza of a hymn (sung by the choir or the congregation).

The 4th Hymn follows the sermon and often its contents correspond to the sermon.

Baptism. The two Sacraments, Baptism and Communion are regarded as part of the Sunday service. Baptisms sometimes take place after the 2nd hymn, but usually after the 4th hymn or after Communion.

The Holy Communion is celebrated at nearly all church services. In the Evangelical-Lutheran view, the service has two poles: Evangelization and the Sacraments. Communion is preceded by the con-

4

fession of Sins and Absolution (or, sometimes they form part of a short service before High Mass). Then the priest says or chants:

Lift up your hearts to the Lord! Let us praise His name. Holy, Holy, Holy is the Lord, God the Almighty, which was, and is, and is to come.

Congregation: *Hosanna in the highest!*

Priest: *Blessed be he that cometh in the name of the Lord.*

Congregation: *Hosanna in the highest!*

The hymn: O Thou, Lamb of God (the Agnus Dei) is sung. (The Danish Hymnal No. 365).

The priest says the following prayer:

O Risen Lord and Saviour who art now Thyself present among us with all the richness of Thy Love! Grant us to receive Thy Body and Blood in remembrance of Thee and confirmation of our faith in the forgiveness of sins. Cleanse us from sin, and strengthen us in the inner man, that through faith Thou mayest dwell in our hearts; make us firm in the hope of eternal life; grant us to increase in love that, together with all who believe in Thee, we may be one in Thee, as Thou art one with the Father!

The congregation answers: *Amen.*

The priest: *Our Father . . .*

The congregation: *Amen.*

The priest speaks the *Words of the Institution,* while the congregation rises:

Our Lord Jesus Christ, in the night in which He was betrayed, took a loaf of bread, gave thanks and brake it, gave it to His disciples and said: Take this and eat it; this is my Body which is given for you. Do this in remembrance of me!

Likewise after the Supper He took the cup, gave thanks, gave it to them, and said: Drink ye all of this; this cup is the New Covenant through my Blood which is shed for you for the remission of sins. Do this, as oft as ye drink it, in remembrance of me! To each communicant, as he receives the bread, the priest says: *This is the Body of Jesus Christ.* And as he drinks the wine: *This is the Blood of Jesus Christ.* To each group of communicants the priest says: *May the crucified and risen Saviour, our Lord Jesus Christ, who hath now given unto you His Holy Body and Blood, wherewith He has wrought satisfaction for all your sins, strengthen and uphold you therewith in true faith unto everlasting life. Peace be with you! Amen.*

Final Prayer. The priest says: *Let us all pray!* and then follows the final prayer, which after Communion is as follows:

We thank Thee, O Lord, our God, Almighty Father, that in Thy mercy Thou hast now refreshed us with these Thy blessed gifts. We beseech Thee that Thou wilt grant that these Thy gifts may duly benefit us, to strengthen our faith, make our hope secure, and to quicken charity in our hearts, for the Sake of Thy Son, Jesus Christ, our Lord.

Congregation: *Amen.*

(In case Communion has not been celebrated another appointed prayer is used).

The Blessing. From the Altar the priest pronounces the Aaronitic Blessing (named after Aaron, Numbers 6, 24–26):

The Lord bless thee and keep thee! The Lord make his face to shine upon thee, and be gracious unto thee! The Lord lift up his countenance upon thee, and give thee peace!

Congregation: *Amen.*

Final Hymn.

Exit Prayer, like the entrance prayer, read by a layman:

O Lord, I thank Thee with all my heart that Thou hast taught me what I shall do. Help me now, my God, through Thy Holy Spirit for the sake of Jesus Christ, that I may keep Thy word in a pure heart, and be thereby strengthened in faith, improved in holy living, and comforted in life and death. Amen.

Organ Postlude.

The cassock was originally the costume of the ordinary citizen, and was given its present form in the 17th century. It is no longer the clergyman's everyday attire, but only worn by him at church services and other sacred functions. With its clerical ruff this clergyman's gown is now, presumably, only to be found in Denmark and Norway.

6

The Chasuble. Before the altar the priest usually wears vestments, i.e. a white surplice and over that a chasuble. In the Danish Church, until the middle of this century, the chasuble was usually red, but now, in many places, the "liturgical colours" have come into use: *white* (1st Sunday of Advent, Christmas, Easter, Trinity Sunday, and all Saints); *red* (Whitsunday and St. Stephen's Day, *i.e.* the day after Christmas); *violet* (Advent and Lent); *green* (all "ordinary Sundays" in the Epiphany and from Trinity Sunday through the rest of the Christian year); and *black* (Good Friday).

Lutheranism does not consider these extrinsic things very important, and there are churches within the Danish Church, where vestments are not used at all.

Those who are even slightly acquainted with the history of the church service will have no difficulty in observing that the Danish church service has many similarities with those of other Churches. A characteristic feature of the Danish Church is the central position given to both evangelization and the Sacraments. With some truth the Danish Church has been described as a "sacramental low church".

The hymns. It is another characteristic feature of the Evangelical-Lutheran service that several parts of the liturgy which used to be sung by the priest or choir have been replaced by hymns sung in the mother tongue. It has been called a "hymnic mass", and Danish Christians dearly love their hymnbook.

Danish Hymnals. The Reformation created a far greater need of hymns than before, and of a hymnbook for the congregation. The first Danish hymnal is the *Malmø Hymnal* of 1528 (Malmø was then within the Danish Realm). Later the most important were: *Hans Thomissön's Hymn Book* of 1569, *Kingo's Hymn Book* (1699), *The Evangelical Christian Hymnal* (1798), *Hymnal for Church and Home* (1897). *The Danish Hymnal,* which is now in use, was authorized by the King in 1953 for use in the Danish churches.

The Hymnal is made up of two parts: one containing 754 hymns with the necessary indexes. The second part contains rituals for high mass, and sacred functions, prayers and texts for all Sundays and holidays, a prayer-book, and, lastly, extracts from Luther's Short Catechism. The Text part is probably not much used, but the hymns are presumably the part of the Church's message which has been most widely welcomed by the Danish people. Since the first edition in 1953 more copies have been printed of the Danish Hymnal than of any other Danish book. On holidays, at the turning-points of men's lives, and for daily devotions the hymnal serves to express individual's praise, thanks, and prayer, and many of the hymns are so firmly rooted in our hearts that they seem unforgettable to Danes.

Experts have told us that the Danish Hymnal is one of the richest in the world. That may not be easy to measure, but this much is certain: both by the piety and poetry of its contents it is one of the finest jewels in the treasury of the Danish Church. So mention must be made of some of our most important hymn-writers: Kingo, Brorson, and Grundtvig.

Thomas Kingo (1634–1703), parish priest of Slangerup, afterwards Bishop of Funen (page 54), wrote 92 of the hymns in the Danish Hymnal, among which are morning and evening hymns and a number of "text hymns", which correspond to the Gospel texts of the Sunday services. His orthodox Lutheran message is stated with manly clarity, his style is fresh and natural. Kingo made a conscious attempt to create a collection of Danish hymns, and his hymns have been important for the evolution of the Danish language.

Among his best-known hymns are: *Now the sun is Rising* (The Danish Hymnal, No. 690), *Sorrow and Joy They wander together* (D. H. No. 41), *Farewell, O World, farewell* (D. H. 525), *Go Stand below the cross of Christ* (D. H. 166), *As the Golden Sun Breaks Through* (D. H. 198). An English translation has been made of: *Come Holy Spirit, Truth Divine* (D. H., No. 258):

> Come Holy Spirit, Truth divine
> and witness bear that Christ is mine
> and that I trust no other name
> To save my soul from sin and shame.

This remarkable granite relief expresses the music of Heaven. It is to be found in the wall of Gamtofte Church in the western part of the island of Funen. This sculpture (its height is almost a metre) represents an angel who, with a rapt expression, is playing a stringed instrument which looks rather like a cross between a violin and a cello. The sculpture, which dates from the last decades of the 12th century, may be a fragment of a larger work. Here reproduced from a stone-rubbing by Mr. Ib Stubbe Teglbjærg.

Above: The Hymnal of Hans Tausen, the religious reformer. Copenhagen 1553.
Below: Hans Thomissøns Hymnal. Copenhagen 1569.

Above: Thomas Kingo's Hymnal. Odense 1689.
Below: Thomas Kingo, 1634-1703 (*vide* page 8).

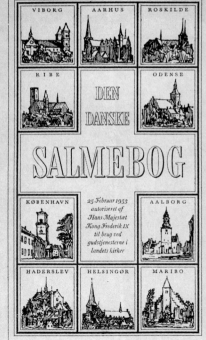

Above: H. A. Brorson: Troens Rare Klenodie (The
Rare Treasure of Faith). Copenhagen 1752.
Below: H. A. Brorson, 1694-1764 (*vide* page 9).

Above: The first Lutheran Liturgical Mass Book
printed in Denmark, 1528.
Below: The Danish Hymnal, Copenhagen 1963.

Above: N. F. S. Grundtvig, 1783-1872 (*vide* page 9 and 62-68)

Below: C. E. F. Weyse, 1774-1842 (*vide* page 17)

Above: B. S. Ingemann, 1789-1862 (*vide* page 16)

Below: Th. Laub, 1852-1927 (*vide* page 17)

Come Holy Spirit, Light divine,
and let Thy light within me shine,
that from the way of God I may
not even for a moment stray.

Come Holy Spirit, from above,
Imbue us with the Father's love
and lend to us Thy voice of grace
to comfort every tribe and race.

Translated by S. D. Rodholm

Hans Adolf Brorson (1694–1764), parish priest of Tønder, afterwards Bishop of Ribe (page 57), was the hymn-writer of the Pietistic movement. He translated a large number of German hymns, besides writing many of his own. The Danish Hymnal contains 60 af Brorson's own hymns and 70 translations. Brorson's translations are, as a rule, of an artistic excellence sufficient to rank as poetic re-creations of the originals. Brorson's hymns bear the stamp of passionate Pietistic fervour, of the call to revival and conversion, and of an unshakeable trust in the grace of God. Brorson wrote a beautiful and straightforward Danish and for mastery of metre has few equals among Danish poets.

Best known among Brorson's hymns are some of those he wrote for Christmas *e.g. In this Sweet Christmas Time* (D. H. No. 90), *The Loveliest Rose has been found* (D. H. No. 98) but there are others worth mentioning: *God's Souls, re-born, to the New Life* (D. H. No. 464), *The White and Heavenly Host We See* (D. H. No. 661), and *Up, Every Thing that God Hath Made* (D. H. No. 12).

Nikolai Frederik Severin Grundtvig (1783–1872) is the greatest Danish writer of hymns. He was chaplain of the Vartov Foundation in Copenhagen, was given the title of Bishop, and was, in many ways, a pioneer of the Church, of education, and the cultural life of the nation (page 62). As a writer of hymns his importance is immeasurable, not merely because of the enormous number of hymns which he wrote (more than 1500, in the Danish Hymnal there are 169 of his own hymns and 101 translations and adaptations), but also because of the linguistic originality, and the depth and wisdom of his piety, which make him unique in Danish – and perhaps in world poetry.

Among Grundtvig's best-known hymns are:

Built on the Rock the Church Does Stand (D. H., No. 280), *Most Wondrous Is of All on Earth* (D. H., No. 277), *All That Which Soars with Upward Flight* (D. H., No. 10), *On the New Jerusalem* (D. H., No. 289). All these hymns have been translated into English:

> Built on the Rock the Church does stand,
> Even when steeples are falling;
> Crumbled have spires in every land,
> Bells still are chiming and calling;
> Calling the young and old to rest,
> But above all the soul distrest,
> Longing for rest everlasting.
>
> Surely in temples made with hands,
> God, the most High, is not dwelling,
> High above earth His temple stands,
> All earthly temples excelling;
> Yet, He whom Heav'ns cannot contain
> Chose to abide on earth with men –
> Built in Our bodies his temple.
>
> We are God's house of living stones,
> Builded for his habitation;
> He thro' baptismal grace us owns,
> Heirs of His wondrous salvation;
> Were we but two His name to tell,
> Yet, He would deign with us to dwell,
> With all His grace and his favour.

Still we our earthly temples rear,
That we may herald his praises;
They are the homes where He draws near
And little children embraces;
Beautiful things in them are said,
God there with us His cov'nant made
Making us heirs to His Kingdom.

Here stands the font before our eyes,
Telling how God did receive us;
Th'altar recalls Christ's sacrifice
And what His table doth give us;
Here sounds the Word that doth proclaim
Christ yesterday, to-day the same,
Yea, and for aye our Redeemer.

Grant then, O God, where'er men roam,
That when the church bells are ringing,
Many in Jesus' faith may come
Where He His message is bringing:
I know mine own, mine own know me,
Ye, not the world, my face shall see:
My peace I leave with you, Amen.

Translated by C. D. Doving   (1837)

Most wondrous is of all on earth
The kingdom Jesus founded.
Its glory, peace, and precious worth
No tongue has fully sounded.

Invisible as mind and soul,
And yet of light the fountain,
Its brightness shines from pole to pole,
Like lights from lofty mountain.

11

Its secret is the Word of God,
Which does what it proposes,
Which lowers mountains high and broad
And clothes the waste with roses.

Let fools against the Kingdom rage
With hatred and derision,
God crowns its reign from age to age,
And brings it to fruition.

Its glory rises like the morn
When waves at sunrise glitter,
Or like in May the verdant corn,
As birds above it twitter.

It is the Glory of the King
Who bore affliction solely,
That He the Crown of Life might bring
To sinners poor and lowly.

And when His advent comes to pass
The Christian's strife is ended,
What here we see as in a glass
Shall then be comprehended.

Then shall the Kingdom bright appear
With Glory true and vernal,
And bring his saved a golden year,
Of peace and joy eternal.

Translated by J. C. Aaberg   (1829)

All that which soars with upward flight
And wings its way towards the light
With notes of joyous singing,
Give praise to God for good is He
And by His grace will set that free
Which still to dust is clinging.

My soul, thou art of noble birth,
Thy thoughts rise upward from the earth
As if on eagle pinions.
Most lofty is thy upward flight
When thou ascendest, robed in light,
To Heaven's fair dominions.

Thou canst not find on land, on sea,
A creature that compares with thee
In need of grace from Heaven;
God verily had thee in mind
When through His Son He saved mankind,
And Thou to Him wert given.

Awake, my soul, lift up thy voice,
Do thou in Christ, the Lord, rejoice
And laud Him as thy Saviour,
Who from the Father's throne above
Bestows on thee His wondrous love,
His grace and ev'ry favour.

Go, tell it to the birds that fly
And to the angels in the sky
Whose song so happy soundeth,
That thou like them with joyful zest
Wilt praise thy God and call Him blest
Whose grace to all aboundeth.

Translated by P. C. Paulsen   (1851)

On the new Jerusalem
Which the King of Bethlehem
By His Word has founded,
We must build with faith and pray'r,
By His Spirit's loving care
And God's grace abounding.

Its foundation prais'd alone
As the Church's cornerstone,
We are all extolling,
It is Jesus Christ, the Lord,
Who a refuge shall afford,
Though the stars be falling.

He who nothing dead condones,
Will of us as living stones
Build His holy temple,
Which upon its base will rise
Like a tree, whose root supplies
It with nurture ample.

Grant, O Lord, Thy Church may rest
On its true foundation blest
And its faith not alter.
Fill it with Thy light and pow'r
With Thy graces it embower,
Never let it falter.

With thy friends, us ever rate,
And despite our lowly state,
Deign with us to tarry.
Let Thy peace in us abide
And, when comes the eventide,
To Thy joy us carry.

Translated by J. C. Aaberg   (1837)

Grundtvig also wrote wonderful Christmas hymns, e.g. *Welcome again God's Angels Small* (D. H., No. 81), and he is sometimes called the Whitsun Hymnist. Among his hymns for Whitsun are: *The Sun in All Its Glory Riseth* (D. H., No. 247), and *O Thou that Come from the Living God* (A Danish adaptation of J. Montgomery's O Spirit of the Living God) (D. H., No. 248).

Besides these three "giants" there are many others worth mentioning. We shall, however, only mention two schoolmasters who have given us beloved hymns. The first was *Hans Christensen Sthen* (1544–1610), author of *Lord Jesus Christ* (**D. H.**, No. 46) which in translation reads as follows:

Lord Jesus Christ,
My Savior blest,
My refuge and salvation,
I trust in Thee,
Abide with me,
Thy Word shall be,
My hope and consolation.

I will confide,
Whate'er betide,
In Thy compassion tender,
When grief and stress,
My heart repress,
Thou wilt redress
And constant help me render.

When I must weep
In sorrow deep
Thy loving care enfolds me.
I have no fear
When Thou art near,
My Savior dear;
Thy saving Hand upholds me.

Lord, I will be
Always with Thee,
Wherever Thou wilt have me.
Do Thou control
My heart and soul
And make me whole,
Thy grace alone can save me.

Yea, help us, Lord,
With one accord
To love and serve Thee solely,
That henceforth we
May dwell with Thee
In jubilee
And see Thy Presence Holy.

Translated by J. C. Aaberg   (1589)

The other was *Bernhard Severin Ingemann* (1789–1862), best
known for his Morning and Evening Songs, *e.g.* *The Sun is Rising
in the East* (D. H., No. 696). Here is a translation:

The sun is rising in the east
It gilds the heavens wide
And scatters light on mountain-crest
On shore and countryside.

It riseth from the valley bright
Where Paradise once lay
And bringeth life and joy and light
To all upon its way.

It greets us from that land afar
Where man with grace was crowned
And from that wondrous morning star
That Eastern sages found.

And from the East God's sun outpours
A heavenly light on earth
A glimpse from Eden's sacred shores
where light and life had birth.

The starry hosts bow down before
The sun that passes them
It seems so like that star of yore
Which shone on Bethlehem.

Thou, Sun of suns, from Heaven come.
To Thee our praises rise
For ev'ry message from Thy home
And from Thy Paradise.*)

Music for the Church Service. Music plays an important part in the service. Of course, the Danish Church has preserved some of this truly international heritage. Both in organ and mass music and in hymn-tunes, the student will recognize much that the Danish Church shares with other Churches. But we have, too, a national treasury of church music. Among its finest jewels are the hymn-tunes. Our great hymn writers have inspired Danish composers, to produce tunes which live in the hearts of the people. Such composers are *C. E. F. Weyse* (1774–1842), *I. P. E. Hartmann* (1805–1900), *N. W. Gade* (1817–1890). A reformer of Danish church singing, and a prolific composer was *Thomas Laub* (1852–1927).

Here are some samples of their compositions:

I Østen stiger Solen op.

C. E. F. Weyse.

1. I Ø - sten sti - ger So - len op, den
spre - der Guld paa Sky, gaar o - ver Hav og
Bjer - ge - top, gaar o - ver Land og By.

(English text page 16).

*) The translations of the Danish hymns are taken from the American Evangelical hymnbook "Hymnal for Church and Home".

Den signede Dag med Fryd vi ser.

C. E. F. Weyse.

1. Den sig-ne-de Dag med Fryd vi ser af Ha-vet til os op-kom-me; den ly-se paa Him-len mer og mer os al-le til Lyst og From-me! Det ken-des paa os som Ly-sets Børn, at Nat-ten hun er nu om-me!

Til Himlene rækker din Miskundhed, Gud!

J. P. E. Hartmann.

1. Til Him-le-ne ræk-ker din Mi-skund-hed, Gud! Din Tro-fast-hed naar di-ne Sky - er; din Ret-færds-haand over Bjer-ge-ne ud er strakt o-ver Da-le og By - er.

Udrust dig, Helt fra Golgata.

N. W. Gade.

1. Ud - rust dig, Helt fra Gol - ga - ta, løft højt det rø - de Skjold; thi Synd og Død, du ser det ja, an - gri-ber mig med Vold!

Alt, hvad som Fuglevinger fik.

Th. Laub.

1. Alt, hvad som Fugle-vinger fik, alt, hvad som ef-ter Fugle-skik med Sanglyd dra-ger Aan-de, lov-synge Gud, for han er god, han i sin Naade raa-der Bod paa Støvets Ve og Vaande!

(English text page 12).

The Ecclesiastical Year. Every Sunday the church bells ring and, in the course of the Christian year, the congregation is led through the great events of the Gospel from Christmas by way of Easter to Whitsun.

In Denmark the holidays of the Christian year are: 1st Sunday of Advent, next 2nd–4th Sundays of Advent, which prepare the way for Christmas. Christmas Day is the proper holiday of Christmas. The Church does not regard Christmas Eve (Dec. 24th) as a holiday, but Danish tradition has made Christmas Eve the occasion for family celebrations in the homes. Usually it includes a short church service in the late afternoon, and this is probably of all the services of the year, the one which draws the largest crowds. Boxing Day is both the second holiday and St. Stephen's Day, commemorating the Church's first martyr.

To the Church New Year's Day is the name-day of Jesus, but, of course, the service also gets its special character from the fact that it is the first day of the calendar year.

Epiphany is often celebrated with a view to the Foreign Mission, the following Sundays lead on to Easter and its holidays. Sunday Septuagesima and Sunday Sexagesima, the five Sundays of Lent and Palm Sunday are the prelude to the Church's greatest event: Easter. Lady Day is not celebrated, but its texts are used on the fifth Sunday of Lent.

The holidays of Easter are: Maundy Thursday, Good Friday, Easter Sunday, and Easter Monday.

The following Sundays are known as 1st–6th Sunday after Easter. The Friday between the 3rd and 4th Sundays after Easter is called "the Great Prayer-Day" or the "Day of Common Prayer". This is a special holiday celebrated only by the Danish Church. It was introduced in the late 18th century when a number of penance and prayer-days were replaced by this one day. Between the 5th and 6th Sundays after Easter, and 40 days after Easter, comes Ascension Day. Ten days later follows Whitsun, Whitsunday and Whitmonday. The Sunday after Whitsun is known as Trinity Sunday, and the next six months are often called the "festival-less" ones, because none of the great events of the Christian year are celebrated in this period.

The Sundays are called by their number after Trinity. The highest number, which can only be reached when Easter comes early, is 27. The first Sunday of November is called All-Saints' Day, but is celebrated both as All-Saints'- and All-Souls' Day and a Memorial Day for the Reformation, which can be said to have been begun on 31st October 1517.

On a suitable autumn Sunday a harvest service is held to give thanks for the year's crops.

We have been sitting in church, attending the service. However, the church houses other activities, too. The reader will find information about these activities on page 99. Now let us have a look round the church. Whether it is old or brand new, its walls and decorations will tell of the life inside this house, record the history of the Danish congregation throughout a thousand years and up to this day. These churches, their history, and especially the life lived in them, will be the subject of the following pages.

CHURCH ARCHITECTURE

A journey through the Danish countryside is essential to the student of that typical exemplar of Danish ecclesiastic architecture, the village church. The landscape is flat with only gentle undulations. The plains with their low, far-away horizons, make on the visitor the impression of being placed under a mighty celestial dome, on whose vault the Danish climate displays its infinite variableness. Scattered here and there among the delicate colours of the chequered fields are the farms, usually surrounded by gardens and trees. Separated by relatively short distances, six or eight kilometres, or even less, nestle the closely built groups of farms and cottages which make up the villages. The wide sky forms an exquisite background for the characteristic, low outline of the village. Its highest points are the chimney of the dairy, the church tower, and to-day the corn silos, poor successors of the beautiful, "Dutch" windmills of former days. Near the cities the sharp demarkation lines between the villages and surrounding fields are being broken by the erection of new dwellings, whose inhabitants go to work in the city. Thus, the limits of the village being effaced, the church's dominating position is lost with the loss of the level fields in front of it. One-family houses and factories spring up like mushrooms.

By and large, however, the Danish village church remains a distinctive feature of the landscape. Whether the journey takes one across the island of Zealand with its red or white, decoratively corbie-gabled, churches or through the length of the Jutland peninsula, whose churches are robust, unsentimental, clearly articulated structures, one is filled with admiration of the skill of the builders who, eight centuries ago, gave these churches their dominant positions. To this day, they not only impress upon the landscape their characteristic stamp, but have also been able to maintain their superiority over all the rest of the architectural features of the countryside, most of which are but a few centuries old. Often, and especially in Jutland, the whitewashed churches dominate their surroundings far and wide. No wonder that many of them have been marked on the charts and serve as landmarks for sailors passing through the Danish seas.

Almost all the churches are orientated in the same east-west direction, and their component parts are the same everywhere, reckoned from the west: the tower, nave, chancel, and, occasionally, the apse. On the south side of the church there was the porch, on the north side, here and there, the vestry and mortuary chapel. The position and composition of the church, might lead one to the mistaken conclusion that all churches are identical. But this is one of the secrets which make these buildings so interesting, so rich in their infinite variety. No two of them are alike. Each has its individual position in relation to the landschape, village, and churchyard. Each has its special space composition which, even when the general plan is identical, nevertheless reveal differences of dimensions, light, and materials. So no one knows the Danish village church till he is familiar with many of them. Then he will be obsessed with them, forever seeking to enter these buildings to meet again the familiar theme in new and thrilling variations. This adventure will be greatly intensified by the study of the details of the church building, not merely of what immediately meets the eye, but also of all that is hidden away in the lofts, above the vaults, and what can be deduced from the study of stones, bricks, mortar, timber, and building techniques. To this we may add the information which at present is being obtained about the wooden buildings which were the forerunners of the stone churches. More and more traces of these wooden churches are brought to light, especially in the strata of earth underneath the stone churches.

THE WOODEN CHURCH

The number of wooden churches must have been very considerable. They were smaller than the stone-built churches, but still had both nave and chancel. Traces of them are often found within the walls of the stone churches. Recent finds underneath the floor of Hørning

Church in Jutland reveal the bay rhythm of their walls. At intervals of about two yards thick oaken poles have been set up with one end dug into the ground. Between these, and immediately above the surface of the earth, a wall plate has been placed. Above this wall plate, and between the posts has been inserted the wall, made up of vertical planks grooved into each other. The top of the wall consists throughout of a horizontal plank, the so-called oar-grummet, resting on all the posts. It serves to combine all the planks at the top, and its ends fit into the corner posts of the church by means of a tenon-and-mortise joints. This mode of construction, applied to the lower part of an outer wall, has been brought to light by investigations in Germany and, curiously enough, has also been found in Norway as a fore-runner of the still existing eight-hundred-year-old stave churches. A fragment of an oar-grummet was found in Hørning Church, in 1887, and has been of signal importance for the understanding of recent finds. The oar-grummet gives information of the construction of the roof, too. A mortise in the upper edge of the plank probably means that, across the church from side to side, have stretched planks, which served as the base of the roof trusses. Information from other sources seem to indicate that the roof was of wood with a covering of shingles, or weather boarding. The oar-grummet also bears ornamental snake carvings and proves that the church was painted in vivid colours. Further, the Hørning finds are interesting because, underneath the wooden church, which dates from the 11th century, there was found a burial mound. It had been of fairly recent date, when the church was built, and contained the body of a woman who had been buried about 1000 A.D. Hørning church, which is built of ashlars, dates from the 12th century. It is interesting, in this identical spot, and within such a short period of time, to find pagan burial customs, a wooden church, and a ashlar-built church. Be it noted, too, that the position of the church was not chance-chosen, but must be due to the already existing of burial mound. In Hørning Church, besides the wooden church, and to the west of it, there were also found port-holes and bits of molten metal, visible proofs that there had also been a separate wooden bell-frame.

The wooden churches were not allowed to stand very long. They were exposed to the dangers of both decay and fire, so they were replaced by the stone churches. The years 1050–1250 mark the most spectacular period of building activities in the history of Denmark. Within roughly two centuries about two thousand churches were built by a population far smaller than to-day's, and without modern technical facilities. This was a unique, nay inconceiveable achievement, a demonstration of admirable energy and self-sacrifice in all classes of the community.

ROMANESQUE CHURCHES

The total number of Denmark's medieval village churches is 1771. Of these 1644 represent the Romanesque style, and 127 the Gothic style. Of the Romanesque churches 186 are late Romanesque brick churches, and 113 of the Gothic churches are brick, 15 granite or other materials.

The fact that most of the churches built in the Romanesque period are still standing cannot but inspire admiration. True, in many cases the Romanesque character of the building is difficult to perceive. This is due to later alterations and additions, most of them dating from the Gothic period. Nevertheless, the eye of the average student of architecture will, in most cases, perceive the Romanesque elements of such a church. In certain parts of the country, especially in Jutland, we find many churches which, to this day, except for the furniture and installations, have retained their original Romanesque character.

By and large, the type of the Romanesque church is the same all over the country. It includes nave, chancel, sometimes an apse at the eastern end, and more rarely a tower. The differences between Romanesque churches are largely due to the building materials, which, of course, vary from district to district. Other differences may be due to varying solutions of the technical and constructional problems. Such variations were caused by the fashions of the day, or by the builders and the artists having been trained at different places.

A visit to a Romanesque church is an interesting experience, and

24

A gateway in the wall surrounding the churchyard gives access to the church, often trough fine old portals. The big gateway is for carriages, the smaller one for pedestrians. Ejsing Church, County of Ringkøbing.

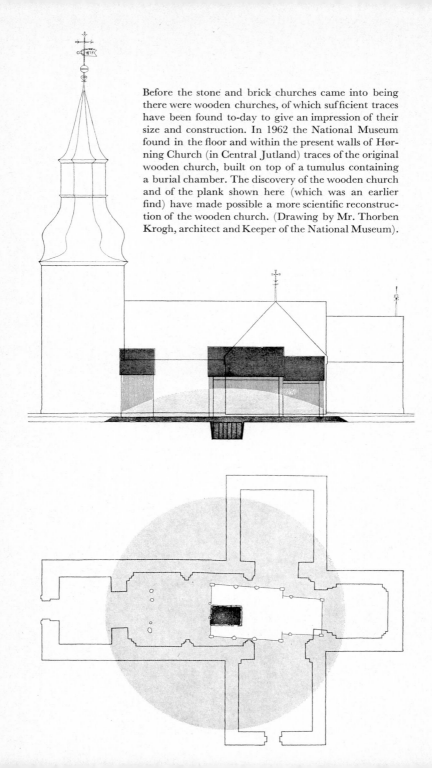

Before the stone and brick churches came into being there were wooden churches, of which sufficient traces have been found to-day to give an impression of their size and construction. In 1962 the National Museum found in the floor and within the present walls of Hørning Church (in Central Jutland) traces of the original wooden church, built on top of a tumulus containing a burial chamber. The discovery of the wooden church and of the plank shown here (which was an earlier find) have made possible a more scientific reconstruction of the wooden church. (Drawing by Mr. Thorben Krogh, architect and Keeper of the National Museum).

The best preserved relic of a wooden church is this fragment of an oak plank found in Hørning Church. It is part of the oar-grummet, the horizontal link between the planks of the wall and the roof. The beautifully carved serpent forms a figure of eight. Its occipital crest and tongue were red, the background yellow and black, the band red with yellow stripes. We have this type of ornament from the middle of the eleventh century.

The earliest stone churches date from the Romanesque period. They consisted only of chancel and nave. Their roofs were covered with wood or lead. The small windows, placed very high on the walls, allowed little light to penetrate into the interior. Hover Church, County of Ringkøbing.

In Sal Church the Romanesque altar ornaments are still preserved. They now hang on the wall behind the altar and serve as a reredos. The so-called "Golden Altars" constitute the climax of Romanesque art in Denmark. (The lower half, originally the altar frontal, is divided into rectangular panels bearing small reliefs representing New Testament scenes. The upper half, with the Romanesque arch (based on a retable) and a crucifix, originally stood on top of the Communion table). The reredos is chased copper, gilt and fixed on a foundation of oak. Sal Church, County of Ringkøbing.

Characteristic features of Romanesque church interiors are their clearly articulated rectangular sections: nave and chancel, covered by grandiose ceilings, some of which have visible beams. Nave and chancel are separated by a Romanesque triumphal arch, which sometimes has niches on either side for the Virgin and the Patron Saint of the church. Maaløv Church, County of Copenhagen.

The baptismal fonts, most of them medieval, are well preserved and still in use, though not for the immersion of infants. The fonts, which are cut in one or two pieces, are often as impressively powerful as that of Rø-gind Church, in the County of Aarhus, shown in this photograph.

Opposite :
Romanesque ashlared churches in Jutland often have fine stone orna-ments, proofs of the high level to which the stone-carver's art had attained. This photograph shows "The Aristocrat's Head" on the apse of Tøm-merby Church, County of Thisted. (Photograph by the National Museum.)

A characteristic feature of the Gothic church interior is the vault, which was built into naves and chancels of the Romanesque churches. Many Gothic wall surfaces, too, were richly decorated with frescoes showing not only biblical scenes and ecclesiastical leaders and events, but also record many secular ones. Besides, these pictures, both in composition and details, tell us amusingly of the clothes and customs of the day. Keldby Church. Island of Møn. Tempera paintings on the vaulting are late 15th century.

The village church as it is usually seen is a Gothic church with porch, vestry, and tower. (There are, nevertheless, a few Romanesque towers). It is either a purely Gothic structure, dating from 1250-1450, or more frequently, an altered and enlarged Romanesque church, whose nave and chancel still constitute a Romanesque nucleus.

Especially in the islands it was costumary to adorn the Gothic churches with corbie steps and panelled gables. The profiles of these panelled walls often produce a play of light and shade which, especially on whitewashed church walls, can be both rich and delicate. Tømmerby Church, County of Holbæk.

Next page:

Romanesque rendering of the crucifixion. Its restraint harmonizes beautifully with the unbroken planes of the interior. One of the most complete specimens of Romanesque frescos is in Raasted Church, County of Randers, where most of the decorations of the east wall of the nave are still preserved. (Photograph by the National Museum).

Gothic crucifixion. The rendering on the curved intrados is highly dramatic, the figures shown in motion. Here, too, we note the harmonious cooperation of ornament and surface. Aastrup Church, island of Falster, County of Maribo. (Photograph by the National Museum).

Modern art, too, is admitted to our ancient churches. In 1954 the old furniture: altar, pulpit, and canopy over the font of Gerrild Church in Djursland, was re-decorated by an artist named Mogens Jørgensen. The colour-scheme was determined by the present light of the church, not by any wish to reproduce the original colour-scheme. Gerrild Church, Djursland, County of Randers, Jutland.

Preceding pages:

1. The church furniture: pews, pulpits, triptychs, reredos, and sepulchral tablets provide rich treasures of the wood-carver's art. This triptych, the work of the younger Abel Schrøder (dating from 1657) is in the auricular style. Præstø Church, County of Præstø.

2. The exuberance and vivacity of the auricular style is manifest even in minute-details. This rendering of The Fall of Man on one of the six panels of the pulpit of Sandby Church is an exquisite example of this style and period (1635). Sandby Church, County of Maribo.

Opposite:

Non-figurative painted ceiling of Hover Church, near Vejle, in Jutland, executed by the artist Mogens Jørgensen 1955.

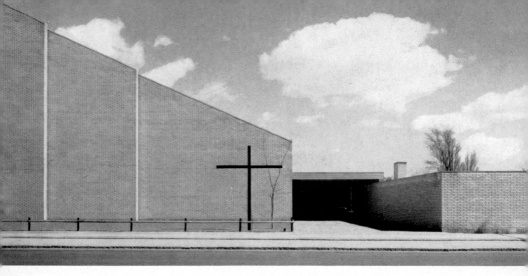

St. Nikolaj's Catholic Church of Hvidovre, near Copenhagen. Architect Johan Otto von Sprechelsen. Both inner and outer walls are yellow brick. The interior is spanned by a hyperbolic paraboloid shell of enforced concrete. 1960.

St. Clement's Church, Randers. Architects: Inger Exner, Johannes Exner, and K. E. Larsen. The Church is situated at the top of a slope in a park on the northern slope of the valley of the Gudenaa River. The building has two storeys, of which the church occupies the upper storey, and the meeting halls the lower one.

Utterslev Church, often called "The Postage Stamp Church" because much of the money for it was made by collecting and selling postage stamps. Architects: Mr. Poul Ernst Hoff and Mr. Bernt Winding. The brick walls are whitewashed. The drapery behind the altar was designed by Miss Barbro Nilsson, Sweden, and executed by John and Kirsten Becker of Copenhagen. 1963.

The Stengaard Church, architects: Rolf Graae and Wilhelm Wohlert. Interior and exterior walls of red bricks, furniture of light-coloured pine. 1963.

The Lundehus Church, Copenhagen, consecrated in 1957. Architect: Holger Jensen.

it becomes still more interesting if, as is often the case, the visitor has first studied a church of the Gothic type. Already at some distance, the Romanesque church reveals its special character. It is not a dominating feature of the landscape. Having no tower, it will only be seen by the visitor when he is quite close to it, a few hundred yards away. Sometimes even it remains invisible till the visitor has entered through the encircling rampart of trees and bushes. This aristocratic seclusion fills the visitor with humility and expectation. At first sight he may exclaim in disappointment, "Is that all!". However, after studying it for a couple of hours, he will go away amazed, because the visit was so rewarding.

Exterior and Wall Technique. Look at the fabric of the church from the outside. If we are in Jutland, the delicate colours of the ashlar walling will fill us with admiration. These delicate shades of colour are due to the individual stones. For they have not, as materials for churches in other countries, come from the same quarry. Each ashlar has been cut out of a boulder collected in the surrounding fields. There the boulders had been left thousands of years before, when the ice retreated after having deposited enormous quantities of stone and earth from various parts of Scandinavia. Some ashlars, of coarse-grained felspar have a marked reddish hue. Others consist of bluish, finer-grained granite with an admixture of quartz. Others again are of multi-coloured porphyries. A walk round the church will, especially when the weather has been damp, reveal a variety of lichens growing on its walls. The yellow circular pattern formed by one of these lichens is particularly beautiful.

Having been shaped with meticulous care, each individual ashlar has strictly rectangular surfaces. The joints are so narrow, and made with such precision, that it is sometimes difficult to insert the blade of a knife. Inside the wall the ashlar has preserved its natural, rounded shape. This does not make for a very stable wall construction, for the stones are liable to slip outward when attacked by dampness and frost.

These walls have a thickness of a yard or more. They are double walls; two walls were built of facing stones, and the interval was filled with smaller stones and chips from the cutting of the ashlars. Over this mixture was poured mortar. This was done gradually, layer by layer, as the double wall grew higher. These walls look substantial, but by modern standards their foundations are of a very poor quality. They are made up of stones, of varying sizes, placed in a foundation-ditch, dug into the ground. The stones are mutually supported by means of wedges and the hollow filled with earth, without the use of mortar. So the foundations are very loosely knit. They move with varying temperatures, and are no less sensitive to changes in the water content of the soil and pressure, caused by drainage, ditches or other similar causes.

The ashlar-built churches of Jutland provide very fine samples of the stone mason's art. Characteristically, the various elements of the building, each according to its special function, was the work of a special artist. This is true of the bases, the north and south entrances, the priest's entrance, window embrasures, pilasters, bases and capitals of the apsides, not to mention the baptismal fonts. These details, often of unique artistic quality, can hardly have been produced on the spot. They were made in special workshops, from which they were ordered, and subsequently put in their places as the building activities progressed.

The Church Interior. When we enter the church, we pass through the porch, a Gothic addition, and find ourselves in a rectangular flat-ceilinged room. Its walls are white-washed, and the windows, provided they are the original Romanesque ones, small and placed very high. Their bevels and rustic walls receive the incoming light and spread it in a soft play of multiple colour strades, producing an effect which is also found in modern church buildings such as le Corbusier's church at Ronchamps. The flat, darkly painted ceiling gives a heavy but harmonious upward conclusion. The characteristic Romanesque arch, which, above the windows, is cut out of one stone, is also found above the chancel entrance, where it has been built of bevelled ashlars. The chancel is smaller than the nave, of almost cubic shape on a square, horizontal plane. If the visitor enters the loft, he may sometimes be rewarded by finding the original roof truss, or part of it. Recent investigations by the National Museum seemingly prove that these remains are much more abundant than was formerly believed to be the case. There seems, too, to have been various types of roof constructions. These roof trusses, being usually made of oak, are often in a very good state of preservation. The Romanesque roof slopes about 45 degrees, less than the slope of the later Gothic roof. This relatively low slope, of course, affects the appearance of the church. It is one of the elements which make for the beautiful, somewhat reserved harmony of the building.

Wall Materials. While the ashlar technique is characteristic of certain parts of Jutland, other churches of the peninsula are built of calcareous tufa, limestone, or tuff, which was imported from more southerly regions. The brick technique came later. The island of Zealand has its own stone wall technique. Instead of finely cut ashlars, the Zealanders split boulders and used them for the double walls. The flat side made in splitting the stone was turned outward. The rounded shapes of the stones make for wider joints than the rectangular Jutland ashlars. This type of wall is easier to keep water-proof, so the masonry is more durable. In Zealand, too, we find tufa, limestone, freestone, and brick in use.

Circular Churches. Special mention must be made of a particular group of Romanesque churches the peculiar circular churches, most of which are found in the island of Bornholm. Space composition: They, too, have nave, chancel, and apse. Only all sections of these buildings have circular ground plans: In Øster Lars Church these sections are joined like soap bubbles sitting on the outside of each other. The nave has three storeys: on the ground floor the main part of the church, then a storage floor, while the third storey was used for defence. The people used these churches as strongholds in times of war. The circular churches did not originally have the conic roofs which we see to-day. Their roofs used to be flat, so they, too, could be used for defence. In their present state, with dark shingle roofs and whitewashed walls, they produce a unique sculptural effect.

Church Furniture. Now let us enter the Romanesque church and, in imagination, visualize its original furniture and ornaments. There is not in existence to-day any church furnished as it then was. To-day's church-goers would never stand for that. With its flat ceiling and the poor light from the small windows, the nave seemed even plainer than it does to-day. There were no pews. Only along the south and north walls seats of masonry for the old and infirm. The other church-goers had to remain standing on the uneven earth floor, or rounded paving stones. There was no pulpit. The only piece of furniture, which must have completely dominated the interior, was the baptismal font. Probably it was given a central position at the most westerly end of the room, astride the centre-line of the nave, in front of the entrance. This large piece of stone sculpture was a utilitarian object, at once plain and richly ornamented, proof of the artist's complete insight into the relations between art, function, and architecture. When the church was not full of people, the font had sufficient power to fill this space. From this demand the artist may have drawn the inspiration which gave these fonts their sculptural power. The baptismal font furnished the west part of the church, and the altar furnished the chancel.

The altar, too, was built of stone, often consisting of granite ashlars or made up of a large stone slap, resting on a central pillar, or on four stone legs. Particularly interesting are the "golden altars", which must have provided magnificent counterparts to the baptismal fonts.

Frescos. Another characteristic feature of the Romanesque church interior is the frescos which cover the walls. Here, too, the artist has been able subtly to adapt himself to the architecture so as not to spoil the proportions and limits of the room. The colours and motifs of the frescos fill the otherwise severe interior with life and joy. The art student will find the detailed study of each motif, the facial expressions and movements of the figures, most rewarding.

Late Romanesque Churches.

Bricks. In the late Romanesque period (in 1170) the bricks became available as a new building material. The three most important groups of brick-built churches are to be found in South Jutland, Vendsyssel, and Lolland-Falster. First of all the churches of the latter islands, attain to a graceful and refined mastery of the decorative use of the qualities of the bricks and the proportions of the stones. The Romanesque arches were decorated with numerous friezes, saw-tooth courses, and dentils on the side walls. On the gable walls exquisite panelled brickwork, whose proportions are naturally subjected to the regularity of the brick bond. The late Romanesque elements constitute a gradual transition to the Gothic period. So it is often doubtful whether a church should be reckoned as belonging to the first or the second of these periods.

THE GOTHIC PERIOD

The Gothic period produced a relatively small number of entirely new churches. However, the Gothic style mainly impressed its stamp upon existing Romanesque churches. Alterations were made both of exteriors and interiors. Sometimes, these alterations were so drastic as to make it difficult at first sight to find original Romanesque masonry. The outward appearance of these churches was changed by a number of additions. A tower was built at the west gable, a porch was added on the south front framing the southern entrance portal, the north wall of the chancel was given a vestry. Furthermore, we often find Gothic side chapels, extensions of chancels and naves. New and larger chancels replace the small Romanesque ones. This is, perhaps, the only really functional alteration.

The Interior. On entering the church, we find a number of equally drastic alterations. Instead of the dark, strictly rectangular flat-ceilinged interior we now find ourselves in a well-lighted room, whose limits are veiled by pilasters bearing one or two severies, and each of which seems to form its own small section of the room. Instead of the flat ceiling, closing the interior above like lid of a box, we now look up into a sort of stone bubbles, whose rounded walls more or less insensibly combine with the vertical walls. Veiling the proportions of the interior, this makes it difficult to get a fairly exact estimate of the height. Thus a light and airy effect is produced. It is enhanced by the light that, through the tall new windows, floods the church. It is a drastic change, and fantastic to see. To-day we admire our modern architecture for the audacity of its concrete shells and arches. How much more worthy of admiration were the technicians of the Gothic period for their shells of masonry and their elegantly built arches, which still endure.

The Gothic church walls, too, were covered with frescos. However, where to-day we see the walls whitewashed, either because the frescos have been destroyed, or because they still remain hidden under the layers of whitewash, we have a special opportunity so study the forms of the vaults, pillars, and arches, and the ever varying interplay of their lines, as we move about the church. The white surfaces can absorb the light, receive the shadows, reflect the light.

We find the same rich play of the light on whitewashed surfaces when we look at the church from the outside. Besides the exquisite details of the corbie-gables and panelled brickwork on the various sections of the building there is the wall surrounding the churchyard, its entrance portals, one for carriages and another for pedestrians. And if, by good fortune, the old whitewashed tithe barn still forms part of the *milieu*, the visit will be an even finer adventure, which the visitor may anticipate as he approaches the church from afar.

Frescos. In the churches where we find the vaults covered with frescos, we can study how the artist allowed the ornaments to spread over the severies. He has, at one and the same time, subjected his art to the convex, irregular intrados and made superior use of them when planning his compositions. All the curved surfaces have been covered with ornaments, and where there was no need for, or possibility of, representational art or biblical scenes, the white surface is covered with flowers, vines, or stars. In this way the artist formed a synthesis of ornamentation and architecture. But it does not make the room seen more harmonious or more easily comprehensible. The artist seems, on the contrary, still further to have intensified the motion and elusiveness which are the architectural effect of the vaults, thus producing still intenser motion, still more elusiveness. The very details, the lines of the figures and the composition, the drama of the motifs, seem to be in motion.

The Romanesque frescos on the vertical and level surfaces of the church were quieter, more restrained, subject to the controlled harmony of the Romanesque style. The Gothic frescos are full of motion elusively emphasizing the continuous character of the Gothic style.

The motifs are of robust realism, but the execution devoid of naturalism. All phases of human life are depicted, the moral no less than the immoral, the biblical as well as the non-biblical, the pious side by side with the superstitious.

Furniture. With the increasing number of priests and celebrants there followed the addition of a vestry, and the necessary extension of the chancel. A consequence of the great expansion of the liturgy was increasing demands for more furniture. The altars took the form of blocks with reliquaries. Further, they must bear the triptychs, often of considerable dimensions. With the triptychs and choir stalls for priests and celebrants wooden furniture and the wood-carver's art gradually penetrated into the church.

The Gothic altar-pieces are triptychs consisting of a centre-panel and two side panels. On certain holidays, the side-panels can be closed so as to cover the centre-panel. By this means, their biblical scenes are concealed, and other illustrations, more suitable for these holidays are displayed on the back of the side-panels. The carvings of biblical scenes found on such triptychs, often magnificent artistic achievements, were produced in the workshops of famous wood-carvers, such as *Bent Notke* of Lübeck and *Claus Berg* of Odense.

THE RENAISSANCE

Buildings. After the Reformation, which in Denmark was introduced in 1536, church building activities almost came to a stand-still. The country already had considerable numbers of churches. Now the new form of worship, the increasing power and vigorous building activities of the aristocracy led to the demolition of almost a hundred churches all over the country. New churches were only built in such localities as had not formerly had any, *e.g.* on some small islands, which had been constantly exposed to enemy raids. The expanding towns, too, required new churches. The churches built in the course of this period are not very characteristic specimens of Renaissance architecture. Then, as now, the Gothic style was regarded as church architecture *par excellence*. So churches were still built with panelled corbie-gables, lancet windows, and buttresses.

In manor-houses and the houses of the wealthy burghers of the towns the so-called "Dutch Renaissance" style won the day. This style is not really very similar to the Renaissance architecture of Holland. With its curvilinear "Italian" gables it is best described as a special Danish development. It is found in a small number of churches in the island of Funen.

Interiors. The Reformation caused changes of the liturgy and a reduction of the number of priests. It gave added importance to the sermon, abolished Latin, and introduced Danish as the liturgical language. There was more hymn-singing, and, generally speaking a more active participation in the service by the congregation. These changes were, of course, of importance for the architecture and, especially, the fittings of the churches.

The pulpit, of which few Gothic specimens have survived, came into extensive use in the Renaissance period. It was placed in the south-east corner of the nave. From there the priest had a good view of the congregation and could make himself heard, while the light from the nearest window fell abundantly on his manuscript. To-day this place for the pulpit has become traditional with us, though architecturally it is far from ideal. It covers much of the east wall of the nave. The stairs often protrude in front of the entrance to the chancel, and where there are vaults, the sounding board is cut to pieces to make room for the severy and groin. Nevertheless, the pulpit still gives us aesthetic pleasure. In our eyes it still has great functional beauty. And it tells us of an important epoch of the history of our Church.

The pulpits were produced in special workshops. In some Danish provinces it is possible to trace the products of various local workshops. This is also true of pews, patrons' boxes, clerks' seats, altars, triptychs, sepulchral tablets, and galleries.

Throughout the Renaissance and Baroque periods we can follow the evolution of the wood-carver's art, for their works adorn many of our churches. Some of the best known wood-carvers were: *Peder Jensen* of Kolding, *Abel Schrøder* of Næstved, *Lorenz Jørgensen* of Holbæk, and *the Holsts* of Køge.

THE BAROQUE AND ROCOCO PERIODS

The influence of the Baroque and Rococo periods on church architecture was no more important than that of the Renaissance. It is the squires' chapels which represent this architectural style. On the other hand, this period produced important, large-scale furnishings of the church interiors. Richly carved altar-pieces, pulpits, and pew-gables adorn many of our churches. Not to mention the often boastfully self-assertive, over-sized, but none-the-less impressive sepulchral tablets on the church walls.

Buildings. In our towns a few churches were built during these periods, *e.g. Our Savior's* in Copenhagen (1696). The Rococo style of the *Christianskirken* (1759) is particularly interesting. It was designed by an architect named *Nicolaj Eigtved.* Its ground plan marks a curious breach with traditional pre-Reformation principles, similar to instances found in Germany. It is built rather like a lecture hall, altar, pulpits, and organ being placed above each other on three storeys on one long side. The remaining three sides have several storeys of galleries, similar to those of a theatre. Even if we have several similar churches, this type of church architecture never became popular in Denmark. The builders of new churches stuck to the traditional longish structure with a centre aisle and with the altar at the end. For acoustical reasons the pulpit was often placed at a considerable distance down one of the long sides. This was not an ideal solution of the acoustic problem for a church in which the sermon had become an essential part of the service. Thus, f. inst., the arrangement of reversible seats in all the pews between the pulpit and altar, are a characteristically unsatisfactory attempt to solve this problem.

NEO-CLASSICISM

Our Lady's, the Christiansborg Palace Chapel, and Hørsholm Church, all by an architect named *C. F. Hansen,* are instances of early 19th century Neo-Classicism. But these churches are most interesting as exponents of the architectural principles of their builder. Neo-Classicism studies and makes use of classical, especially ancient Greek, elements.

THE PERIOD OF ECLECTICISM

The next century proved unable to evolve an independent style in Church architecture. For churches, as for secular architecture, the usual recourse was the imitation of historical styles. This imitativeness was characteristic of the vigorous church building activities, which, especially in Copenhagen, were due to the rapid expansion of the city.

For centuries Copenhagen had been nestling within its walls. Once these limits had been passed, extensive and densely populated quarters sprang up: Østerbro, Nørrebro, and Vesterbro. Blocks of tenements were built by jerry-builders, but no churches. So a group of private individuals started *The Copenhagen Church Fund* (vide page 107, 150) for the purpose of dividing up the new districts of the city into parishes, each with a maximum population of 10.000. Large sums were collected, and the Fund's first churches date from the turn of the century: the Apostles' Church, Brorson's Church, Elijah Church, Luther's Church, etc. Of these churches the last two were designed by *Martin Nyrop,* the builder of Copenhagen's City Hall. The architect of the Apostles' Church was *V. Koch.* It is a small, well-proportioned imitation basilica. What makes it especially interesting is the fact that it was built within a large block of flats, behind the houses that face the street. As a visible indication that here was a church, the belfry was built in line with the street frontage, its only connecting link with the church being a roofed passage. In recent years all the back premises of this block have been demolished. A spacious courtyard has been created, which provides the street frontage houses of the block with light and air. For one thing, the demolition of these premises set a good example of slum clearance, while on the other hand the form given to this courtyard might have been happier. Of greater interest, however, is the fact that it has brought this obscure little church into full daylight. The Elijah Church in Vesterbro's Square was built into the street frontage. With its two towers it is an imitation of the interesting medieval church of Fjenneslev in Central Zealand.

Transitional Church architecture. Mention must be made of a transitional type, or rather of the church that marked the end of the period of eclecticism. It is the absurdly over-dimensioned Grundtvig's Church on Bispebjerg. It was built to the design of *P. V. Jensen Klint,* and is especially remarkable for excellent use of the fine texture and beautiful details of a yellow, handmoulded brick. Unfortunately, Grundtvig's Church is not very suitable for the divine service.

Far better and more moderate is the Bethlehem Church, which is situated in Aaboulevarden. It was designed by Kaare Klint, professor of architecture, and the son of P. V. Jensen Klint. Like all Klint's other works, the Bethlehem Church was planned with quite definite proportions. All the individual bays are alike, which is obtained by increasing all surfaces and linear measurements by $\sqrt{2}$ series. This church is another example of beautiful texture and details.

RECENT CHURCHES

To-day the total number of churches built by "The Copenhagen Church Fund" is about fifty, and it probably has plans ready for another fifty. However, to-day's strict building restrictions have, for the time being, considerably hindered church building activities. The rapidly expanding residential districts on the outskirts of Copenhagen require a considerable number of new churches. The popularity of these plans for new churches is most clearly shown by the initiative taken by a group of inhabitants of Bidstrup, who, with their own hands, built the first part of a block which was to consist of a church and subordinate buildings. Following this lead, similar building activities are being started in other localities.

The new churches which are being built to-day are not eclectic. Like other modern buildings, they are designed in accordance with to-day's ideas of architecture, which stress function, and honesty of construction and materials. Moreover, honest attempts are being made to keep in mind that the church is, too, a centre of welfare work.

Holger Jensen, an architect who has designed quite a few of the recently built churches, was also the builder of the interesting little Lundehus Church. This church is situated in a residential district made up of three or four storeyed blocks of flats. In this environment it is impossible for at modest little church to assert itself by its dimensions. It can, however, do so by its form. So the architect built the small church on a square ground plan and covered it with a pyramidal roof, in whose open top the church bell hangs. This body, whose shape is an adaptation of that of a buoy, is surrounded by meeting halls, which can be combined and opened into the church so as to make possible meetings and services with varying attendances.

Typical of these new churches is the builders' requests that, besides the church, there be halls for various kinds of meetings, including the work among the young people. Sometimes the architect is asked to provide within the same block a kindergarten, a youth club, and a day nursery. Of course all these requirements greatly influence the appearance of the building. The creation of a harmonious church interior becomes most difficult when there must also be possibilities of adding to it one or two adjoining halls. This problem has found an excellent solution in Stengårdskirken by architects *Rolf Graae* and *Wilhelm Wohlert*. The adjoining halls are placed along one of the long sides of the church, but made less conspicuous by the gallery above. The materials used give a peaceful and harmonious effect, dominated by red "Helsingborg" bricks and light-coloured, undressed pine wood.

Among recently built Copenhagen churches worth mentioning there is also the latest of the Roman Catholic churches. This is St. Nicolaj's in Hvidovrevej, designed by *Johan Otto von Spreckelsen*. The Catholic Churches do not require the addition of meeting halls, so it is possible for the architect to concentrate on the creation of a purely church interior. Here the church interior is surrounded by almost unbroken walls and covered by a concrete shell in the shape of a hyperbolical paraboloid, tipped in such a way that its lower end is over the entrance corner, and its higher end above the altar. It receives the light through two narrow openings to the left of the altar, thus emphasizing the height of the church interior. It is interesting to find a Catholic church built on an almost square plan, with the altar placed in one corner, and the congregation grouped round it in an arrangement of pews shaped like a 90-degree sector of a circle. Originally, the pews were arranged without a central gangway. By its plan and interior St. Nicolaj's is strongly reminiscent of some church structures produced in post-Reformation Germany in an attempt to invent a new Protestant type of church. Like the other churches here mentioned, St. Nicolaj's is made beautiful by the honest use of the textures of such materials as yellow brick, oak, and pine.

The suburb of Utterslev has recently got its own church, Utterslev

Church, built by architects *Hoff* and *Vindinge*. Its form is essentially different from those of other Copenhagen churches. Above the altar, the roof has been raised to let the light pour in on the altar through a tall window.

Among recently built provincial churches mention should be made of Bolbro and Munkebjerg Churches in Odense, both designed by the brothers *Knud* and *Ebbe Lehn Petersen*. The Jutland town of Esbjerg has got a new church, Trinity Church, the work of architects *Knud Thomsen* and *Erik Flagstad Rasmussen*. The cruciform roof of this church ends in four triangular glass gables, which are gradually being replaced by stained glass mosaics, one of which has already been completed by the artist *Urup Jensen*.

On the sloping north bank of the Gudenaa River, in a park belonging to the municipality of Randers, architects *Inger* and *Johannes Exner* and *Knud Erik Larsen* have just completed the construction of a new church. There is, from the site, a fine view of the river valley. This and the steep slope have been decisive factors for the design of the church. The two-storeyed building stands at right angles to the slope. The entrance to the upper storey, which contains the church, is from the street, while the entrance to the meeting halls in the lower storey is from a terrace below. The width and height of the church are increased in the direction of the altar, so that its dimensions are largest in this spot. There is, too, the greatest concentration of light, the wall behind the altar being divided up into tall, slender brick pillars, reaching from floor to ceiling. Between these pillars glass panes have been inserted, giving a distant glimpse of the remote "river-scape". In the construction of this church, too, the choice of high-quality building materials, and the desire for homogeneity have been decisive factors. So yellow bricks have been used, and undressed wood-work inside. The outside wood-work has got the grey-green colour of the impregnation. The demand for extra space has been met at the back, so as to avoid a large opening in the side of the church. The altar is still waiting for the stained glass mosaic which is to replace the temporary red plate glass.

The architect *C. F. Møller* has designed Aarhus' Møllevang

Church, which is situated on a slope, too. Light only being admitted through a circular window in the flat roof over the altar, the interior of the church is somewhat dark. The meeting rooms are in the lower storey. In the church itself there is no possibility of adding extra space. The church is built of red brick.

In many places the church committees have building projects in readiness for the day when the Government will grant building permits. Many of these projects have been submitted for competitions. The number of projects submitted bear witness to the great interest of the architects. One of the latest was an international church architecture competition arranged by the Church Ministry. The first prize went to a Norwegian architect, *Helge Hjertholm*.

Several attempts are being made to introduce modern art into churches, even medieval ones. The National Museum has taken the matter in hand with praiseworthy energy. A painter named *Mogens Jørgensen* has produced interesting glass mosaics for several old churches. He has also produced fascinating ornaments on woodwork and ceilings. Interesting line ornaments on the pulpit, altar-piece, and font of Gerrild Church have been made by Mogens Jørgensen and his wife, *Gudrun Stenberg*. A fine ceiling in Hover Church, near Vejle, was the exclusive work of Mogens Jørgensen.

Financing the New Churches. The funds necessary for church projects are obtained partly by private contributions, partly through loans from public banks, and partly through Government grants. The Government grants usually amount to one third of the total expenditure, the maximum grant being kr. 300.000. The amounts of the loans must be proportionate to the amounts contributed by individual donors. No Government grant is given for the meeting halls, unless they constitute an integral part of the church itself.

Sometimes the new churches have been called experimental, and it has been said that no new ecclesiastical style of architecture has, so far, been invented. Such a statement must at present seem premature, the perspective being, as yet, too short. We are still too close in time to these new churches. But, keeping our new churches in mind, let us cast a backward glance at the Period of Eclecticism, Neo-

Classicism, the Rococo, Baroque, Renaissance, and Gothic periods, and the Romanesque churches, and we will see a diversity of church-types, as different as can be. Indeed, the differences are far greater than between the new churches of to-day. And be it noted, all these churches are in use to-day, and seemingly satisfactory. The multiplicity of types is not undesirable, on the contrary, it is a valuable record, for better or for worse, of the history of the Danish people, in days of peace and in times of war. The study of eight centuries of church building will reward the student with a unique insight into the Danish national character.

HISTORY OF THE DANISH CHURCH

The birth certificate of the Danish Church is preserved in the village of Jelling, to the west of Vejle, in Jutland. A large boulder, weighing about a ton, bears the following runic inscription:

King Harald ordered these memorial tombs to be made for Gorm, his Father, and Thyra, his Mother, the Harald who conquered all Denmark and Norway and made the Danes Christians.

This Harald, with the nick-name *Blue Tooth,* ruled Denmark 940–985. About 960 he officially adopted the Christian faith and was baptized. Then, in the words of a Saxon chronicle he "commanded the peoples over whom he ruled to leave their false gods".

THE MISSION PERIOD

This event was preceded by a period of preparation lasting several centuries. During this period the Danes had become acquainted with Christianity, partly by chance, and partly through the activities of missionaries coming from the south.

Increasing trade and, no less, the vikings' raids on the countries to the south and west, gave the inhabitants of Denmark an impression of the Christian faith, which soon began to influence them. When the vikings robbed churches and monasteries, they not only possessed themselves of many treasures. Often they could not avoid feeling the spiritual power emanating from such places. Some of them were even baptized, and this fact, that "White Christ" was victorious over the unconquerable, may have been accepted in their countries as the strongest evidence of His power. Following their usual way of thinking, the old Northmen did not primarily seek the True God, but the strongest, the one who could fill their lives with the richest blessings.

These events prepared the way for the direct Christian mission. After an unsuccessful attempt, made already about 735 by Willibard, apostle of the Frisians, the mission was begun in 823, when Louis le Débonaire sent Ebo, archbishop of Reims, with many attendants to Hedeby, a trading centre close to the modern town of Slesvig. Here he preached and entered into negotiations with several Danish kinglets – rulers of parts of the country. Three years later, one of them, Harald Klak, was obliged to take refuge at the court of the Emperor Louis at Ingelheim, where he was baptized.

When, shortly after, Harald Klak returned to Denmark, one of his attendants was the man who was to become the Apostle of the North. This was *Ansgar,* a monk from the monastery of New Corvey on the river Weser. Faced with terrible difficulties – once, f. inst., the vikings robbed his house in Hamburg – Ansgar strove tirelessly until his death, in 865, to spread the Christian message in the districts of Hamburg and Bremen, in Holstein, Friesland, and Scandinavia. On the whole, however, the results were meagre, especially among the Danes, although, besides religious zeal, Ansgar possessed both practical common sense and diplomatic tact.

The energetic, race-proud, and extrovert Danes may not have found the type of Christianity which Ansgar represented very attractive. His was the "tearful piety" characteristic of monastic life in France and Germany, *i.e.* a Christianity which constantly dwelt upon the agony and death of Christ, exhorting the faithful to lives of poverty and asceticism, and calling upon them to love God, to do penance, and to turn their gaze inwards for pious contemplation. All this accompanied by pious visions, the hearing of heavenly voices, and contemplation of the approaching doom, which was eternally to separate the damned from the penitents.

Nevertheless, a few converts were made. In the century that separated the death of Ansgar and the baptism of Harald Blue Tooth the new faith spread insensibly without giving rise to the wars that occurred in so many other countries.

But it was the baptism of King Harald Blue Tooth which gave the Christian Church an officially recognized status in the kingdom. Since it is characteristic of the spirit of the age, mention must be made of the immediate cause of the King's conversion. At a feast a quarrel arose in the presence of the King as to whether Christ or the other gods were strongest. A Christian bishop named *Poppo* maintained that there was only one True God, the Father, and His only begotten son, Our Lord Jesus Christ, and the Holy Ghost, while the other gods were demons, not gods. To prove his assertion, Poppo the next morning went through the ordeal of carrying red-hot irons. As he got through it unscathed, the King was prepared to be baptized.

THE CHANGE OF CULT AND RELIGION

The above-mentioned scene makes it clear that what appealed to the Danes was not the "Tearful Piety" of the continental monasteries, but the English conception of Christ as the Victorious King, who invades the realm of Death and plants his banner in it. This Christ, the Victor, was able to win the people from whom the vikings had sprung. And there were other reasons, too, which made it a natural thing for us to come under Anglo-Saxon influence. For just after the death of Harald Blue Tooth contacts between England and Denmark were very close. Harald's son, *Swein Forked Beard,* made conquests in England, and afterwards *Canute the Great* founded his Anglo-Scandinavian Kingdom. In spite of the fact that officially the Danish Church was part of the archbishopric of Hamburg-Bremen, it received its richest impulses throughout the early Middle Ages from England. One reason for this was the long line of bishops and monks sent to us across the North Sea.

In the centuries immediately after the death of Harald Blue Tooth, Christianity spread throughout the country. Many wooden churches, and the first stonebuilt ones, were built. About 1060 *King Swein Estridsen* divided up the country into nine dioceses (to the old dioceses of Slesvig, Ribe, Odense, and Roskilde were added new ones in Aarhus, Viborg, Vendsyssel, Lund, and Dalby, − the last two in Scania, now the most southerly province of Sweden, which was Danish until 1669).

But what was more important, the old Nordic religion was supplanted by Christianity − but slowly, and by no means completely.

Ever-increasing numbers were baptized and promised to worship

Christ as their God. Many however, did not think it advisable to cut off their contacts with the forces of nature which had hitherto ruled their lives, so they secretly went on worshipping the deities which they believed dwelt in trees, springs, and curiously shaped stones.

Add to this that not a few of their old ideas found their way into the new faith, or could easily be adapted to objects similar to those with which they had formerly been associated. Hitherto, believing in Thor, God of Thunder, who with his hammer vanquishes the giants, enemies of mankind, they had used a T-sign, reminiscent of the hammer, to bless with. Now this T-sign was given up in favour of the Christian cross – outwardly a very slight change. The pouring of water which had hitherto marked the adoption of the new-born child into the family, was replaced by baptism, and Holy Communion replaced the communal meal eaten in the sacrificial sanctuary. The first priests were far from wishing to make the change too abrupt: where, formerly, the image of Frey, the fertility god, had been carried about the fields to secure the year's crops, the priests now carried the crucifix and images of the saints in solemn procession. At the communal meals, the sacrifical feasts, the climax had been the dedication of a memorial cup, when the wish was pronounced that the year might be peaceful and good for the country. This custom was preserved, too, but Christianized, the cups now being consecrated to Our Lady or Saint Michael. The old gods were driven out, but there remained numerous of relics of popular belief, such as goblins, trolls, mermen, etc. Some of them have lingered on in popular superstition to this very day.

And yet what had taken place was not merely a change of cult –, but also a change of faith. An entirely new attitude had come into being. The customs of the people proved that new moral standards had been set up. To the old Northmen it had not seemed barbarous to expose unwanted babies in the wilderness and leave them to perish there. For according to the primitive way of thinking, babies were not alive until by a ceremony they had been adopted into the family. Now the church taught the Northmen that, in the eyes of

God, all human beings are equally valuable, the deformed and the weaklings no less than the healthy and the vigorous.

Gradually this and other survivals of paganism, which obviously disagreed with the Christian way of thinking, were suppressed. The family-feuds died down, the slaves were set free, the fate of prisoners of war became less appalling. To all who worked the holidays of the church became welcome breaks in the working-days' monotony.

Of course, the Christian doctrine of neighbourly love must have given offence to many Northmen. However, gradually they began to realize that one's neighbour is not only one's relative, comrade-at-arms, or countryman, but also the enemy one is fighting. It was difficult to accept this ideal of humanity and meekness and to submit to the demand for fasting and chastity. For a long time to come, important men, who in other respects were friends of the church, refused to give up their concubines. The command to chastity seemed downright immoral to men who had been brought up to regard the continuation of the family as a fundamental duty. To submit to the demand for celibacy meant exclusion from one's family. But gradually the new ideas were generally accepted. More and more came to feel blessed by the meeting with "White Christ", whether it took place in a humble house of worship built of timber, or behind the impregnable walls of a high-ceilinged church.

ORGANIZATION OF THE MEDIEVAL CHURCH

At the beginning of the 12th century the Danish Church developed into a fully organized part of the universal Catholic Church, and throughout the Middle Ages its development, in many respects, ran parallel to what we know in other European countries.

As in other Germanic countries, relations between Church and King gave rise to many problems. True, the Church was Roman Catholic, and directed from Rome. But it was also a National Church, ruled by the Danish King. Now it was not part of Germanic juridical ideas for the King without a blow to resign his position as Head of his Church and master of his own clergy. The King's attitude became even more intransigent when, in the course of the 13th century, the feudal system gradually made archbishops, bishops, and abbots vassals of the King, imposing upon them the duties of attendance on him and of military service in times of war. While the Church insisted upon its sovereignty, the King maintained, that the fiefs were his property, which he could give to laymen and clerics at will. The claim of the Church to be an independent proprietor of land was fundamentally foreign to a Germanic prince, – to whom it seemed a matter of course that the property rights must be vested in persons, not institutions. Foreign, too, were the ideas that the Church had a right to tithes of all crops, and that clerics should be exempt from the royal jurisdiction, and be subject to canonical law only. On the contrary, to the Danish King it was a matter of course that the owner of the church and the church land possessed, too, the right to appoint the clergy and provide for them. The clash of these Germanic principles with the claims of the Roman Church, which took the form known as Gregorianism, led to many explosions. In the course of time the Church suceeded in obtaining the fulfilment of many of its claims, but not without conflict. The evolution was most happy for both the Danish Kingdom and the Church when, recognising the King's rights, the clergy was able to co-operate with the temporal authorities, but equally unfortunate whenever the two parties quarrelled. Medieval Denmark knew both situations.

As an early example of how the King tried to make use of the Church to fortify his own position may be mentioned that in 1101 the Crown succeeded in obtaining the canonization of King Canute, who, fifteen years before, had been murdered in Odense Cathedral by rebellious peasants, whom he had infuriated by his highhanded tax-policy. However, this canonization failed to produce the desired effect. St. Canute never became a popular saint in Denmark. The memory of his misdeeds was too fresh in the people, and soon the Church got leaders who made it quite clear that they did not want to see the Church harnessed to an increasingly powerful Crown.

When, in 1104, the Danish Church was freed from the supremacy of Hamburg-Bremen it was in a far better position to shape an independent policy. A Scandinavian archbishopric was established

46

in Lund, which, as already mentioned, at that time was within Danish territory. In 1152 Nidaros-Tronheim in Norway, and in 1164 Upsala in Sweden were separated from Lund as independent Archbishoprics. The Archbishop of Lund in the years 1137–1177 was *Eskil,* one of the greatest personalities in Danish history. Inspired by Gregorian ideas, he asserted the Church's independence of the temporal power. This led to war: on several occasions he had to spend years in exile. However, he succeeded in realizing several of his ideas of Church-policy, and at the same time in laying the foundation of a durable and harmonious co-operation of Church and Crown.

In the course of the 12th century the independence of the Church was consolidated by the introduction of tithes and the foundation and growth of chapters. Church lands were extended and gradually freed from taxes and other tributes to the Crown. At length, too, it was accepted that the clergy should be exempt from temporal jurisdiction. Thus the Church grew up to be the richest and most powerful institution in the country beside the Crown.

At the same time an internal consolidation took place, largely inspired by Clunyacensian ideas and bearing the stamp of *Bernardine* piety. New Churches were built throughout the country, and the old ones were enlarged and more richly decorated. Stricter moral standards were imposed upon the clergy, e. g. with regard to celibacy. Many new monasteries were set up, especially by the Cistercian and Premonstratensian orders.

Eskil's work was continued by Bishop *Absalon,* also known as the founder of the city of Copenhagen. With King *Valdemar the First* he vanquished the Wends, North German pirates, who had long been making inroads on the long coastlines of Denmark. This close co-operation of Crown and Church was continued by Absalon's successors as archbishops, for the good of both parties, until the end of the 13th century. During this period several "crusades" were launched against pagan countries south of the Baltic, e.g. Estonia. During one of these raids, the legend has it, Dannebrog, the red banner with the white cross, was sent to the Danes from Heaven –

a tangible symbol of the close co-operation of Church and Crown. Soon the new orders of mendicant friars found their way to Denmark. In 1223 the Dominicans started their activities, in 1232 they were followed by the Franciscans. At a time when the Papacy, under Innocence III, tried to establish the absolute supremacy of the Church, the Danish Church unconditionally recognized the King as ruler of the country. He was the master of the laws, which must, certainly, be accepted by the people. He it was, too, who administrated justice, and ruled the country through his officials. His authority to exercise these functions had not been granted him by the Church. It came to him direct from God, and among his most important duties was the protection of the Church from the inroads of laymen. In the late Middle Ages King and Church stood side by side, but by acknowledging the King as its Protector in the temporal sphere, the Church recognized that, in this sphere, it was his subject. This idea was most clearly expressed in the Jutland Law, passed in 1241, a year before the death of King *Valdemar* the *Victor*.

That year marked the end of a century of progress and success for both the Church and the State. The history of the subsequent century is one of harrowing quarrels between the Kings and their vassals, both laymen and clerics. Incompetent Kings gradually played large parts of the Danish territory into the hands of North German noblemen and financiers. The archbishops, *Jacob Erlandsen* and *Jens Grand* pursued a Church-policy, which must needs add to the internal disruption of the country. In the end the kingdom was completely dissolved, and there followed a kingless period (1332–1340).

In the reigns of King *Valdemar Atterdag,* so called because with his coming to the throne a new day dawned over the country, (1340 –1375) and of Queen *Margrethe* (1375–1412) the monarchy was slowly re-established. Its structure underwent considerable changes, chiefly due to the growth of the towns. A self-assertive citizenry came into being, but for a long time remained largely dependent of the North German Hanseatic League.

The larger of the two runic stones of Jellinge in the Jutland peninsula, bearing Scandinavia's oldest picture of Christ – the birth-certificate of the Danish Church (*vide* page 41).

The oldest crucifix in Denmark, dating from about 1100 (Åby Church, near Århus). Note how the old Scandinavians portrayed Christ: a bearded King of the vikings with a crown on his head. No trace of Christ's agony on Golgatha. It is Christ the Victor, who vanquished Death that the artist wished to portray. The figure stands in front of the cross with open eyes. The feet are placed one beside the other without being nailed to the cross. The arms are stiffly stretched and do not bear the weight of the body.

This crucifix (from Elmelunde in the island of Møn, about 1350) is entirely different from the one shown on the preceding page. This is Christ's Passion: the body
is convulsed with pain and terribly emaciated. His head is hanging down on one
side, and the facial expression is one of intense suffering. The kingly crown of the
older crucifix has been replaced by a crown of thorns. His legs are crossed, the feet
pierced by a nail, both arms and legs thin with sharp outlines. A terrifying rendering of the horror of death.

Renaissance-style pulpit, dating from about 1589 (Vindinge Church, near Roskilde in the island of Zealand). The friezes surrounding the uppermost inscription are derived from Greek temples, as also the capitals of the pilasters above the corner figures, and several other details. Both corner figures shown by the photograph represent Christ: one holds the royal orb, the other the cross. The large panels between these figures are decorated with reliefs. The one to the left shows the baptism of Christ: John The Baptist pouring baptismal water out of a jug over the head of the Saviour, while the Dove is hovering above. The next panel represents a Protestant church service. The preacher is dressed in non-clerical clothes, and in front of the pulpit are groups of church-goers, the women seated, the men standing.

The picture gives an impression of the essence of the Evangelical church service *viz.* the celebration of the two sacraments and preaching of the gospel. The altar bears a crucifix, and both alb and chasuble are in use.
(Altar-frontal of Thorslunde church, 1561, now in the National Museum, Copenhagen).

Next page:
Claus Berg's masterpiece, the magnificent triptych of *Sanct Knuds Kirke* (St. Canute's Church) at Odense in the island of Funen. Originally meant for *Graabrødre Kirke* (the Grey Friars' Church) which King Hans had chosen to contain his tomb. At the top of the central panel the celestial coronation of the Virgin, immediately below the men of the Old Covenant and the Apostles. The next row shows a number of saints, and at the bottom St. Anne hands the Christ-Child to Mary, while female saints are looking on. The two wings show numerous scenes of the life of Christ. Below on predella kneels King Hans and Christian II with their queens and children. Claus Berg, supreme among medieval wood carvers, was born in North Germany, but spent the first three decades of the sixteenth century working at Odense. His naturalistic and vividly dramatic Gothic figures are found in many churches.

M. JOH. TAUSSANUS
Daniæ Reformator et Episcopus Ripensis
Symb. Ægyptus homo est non Deus fortis.

Hans Tausen, 1494-1561 (*vide* page 52).

Petrus Palladius.

Peder Palladius, 1503-60 (*vide* page 53).

LVDEWIG HOLBERG
FREY-HERR VON HOLBERG.
geb. 1684. gest. d. 24. Febr. 1754.

Ludvig Holberg, 1684-1754 (*vide* page 57-58).

J. P. Mynster, 1775-1854 (*vide* page 61-62).

NICOLAUS HEMMINGIUS.

Hunc merito observat Doctorem Ecclesia fidum
Qui ordine perspicuus, dulcis et eloquio
Et Verbo et Vita docuit qui pascere. Felix
PASTORE HEMMINGI pascere qui didicit.

Cum privil.

Niels Hemmingsen, 1513-1600 (*vide* page 53-54).

IOHANNES EGEDE

Hans Egede, 1686-1758 (*vide* page 56).

Søren Kierkegaard, 1813-55 (*vide* page 68-72).

Olfert Ricard, 1872-1929 (*vide* page 78).

Vilh. Bech preaching at Ubby Church, drawing by Mads Jepsen (*vide* page 75-76).

N. F. S. Grundtvig listening to the hymn-singing at Vartov Church, his young son by his side (painting by C. Dalsgaard, 1868),

From the Grundtvigian Folk High Schools:
Above: Ludvig Schrøder, first principal of Askov High School, lecturing.
Painted by Erik Henningsen 1902.
Below: Ernst Trier speaking at Vallekilde High School. Drawing by Viggo Pedersen.

At the same time the country developed into what was more clearly a national state, ruled by the King and the Council of the Realm. At a time when the central authority of the Catholic Church had entered upon a period of rapid decline, marked by a preoccupation with material interests and the almost total lack of spiritual authority, the leaders of the Danish Church felt called upon to play an active part in interior policies of the country, in order thereby to safeguard the Church's and their own interests. Often the highest posts were given to nobles, and frequently the Church had to endure the interference of King and Council in its affairs. In many respects, however, and just because of this close co-operation between the authorities of Church and State, the closing years of the Middle Ages were a period of rich growth for the Church. New churches were built, especially in the rapidly growing towns, and many village churches were rebuilt and enlarged. From Sweden came the Bridgetine Order, and in 1479 the University of Copenhagen was founded, primarily as a school for priests.

SPIRITUAL DEVELOPMENTS WITHIN
THE MEDIEVAL CHURCH

By and large, the spiritual life of the Danish Church in the Middle Ages developed along the same lines as in other countries. The monasteries became centres of important welfare work, and also of cultural work in literature, medicine, jurisprudence, etc.

In the 12th and 13th centuries the Church in Denmark, as elsewhere, became the spiritual home of the people. She offered security and harmony in an otherwise insecure world. The mass was, of course, the usual Roman one, but frequently, and especially in the last centuries of the Middle Ages, sermons were preached in the native tongue. We preserve, as little gems of our, otherwise meagre, medieval literature, a few songs in praise of the Virgin. And we have, too, some attempted translations of the Bible into Danish. Not very successful attempts, but still the work had begun.

We have much evidence of the importance of the Sacraments, and of the influence of the, often quite fantastic, lives of the saints. It will be found that foreign saints appealed to the minds more successfully than the specific Danish ones. *Canute Lavard* (murdered near Haraldsted in 1132) became no more popular a saint than St. Canute. Of the Scandinavian saints, stout-hearted Norwegian *Saint Olav* became most popular. Besides other evidence of his popularity we have the church frescos. The Danish ballads – the jewels of our medieval literature – show how much of the popular beliefs had lived on in the minds of the people, far into the age of Catholicism. Here we meet with the secret powers of nature, which have remained very much alive. Mermaids, elves, bewitched virgins, magic runes and formulas tell us of a world which had not lost its hold upon medieval man. But we feel, too, how, in the course of time, the Christian Faith strengthens its hold upon the minds. Before the knight's cruciform sword the wicked elves must flee, and the mention of the name of Christ paralyses the evil powers.

In Denmark, too, the late Middle Ages was a period of fear and spiritual insecurity. The Church had lost its position as the undoubted centre of life. The Clergy, often deservedly, was criticized and sapped the people's trust in the Church. Again and again it was seen how the preachers of the Christian Religion betrayed the ideals they had been sent to inculcate.

This drove some to scepticism. Others found in mysticism the way to communion with God, not in the Church but in the inmost recesses of their own souls.

Nevertheless, the number of those who broke away from the Church was small. To the majority the Church remained God's instrument for the salvation of souls. The fear of death, which at the time was whipped up to unnatural heights, drove many into the arms of the Church. The terror was increased by the prospects of the tortures of Purgatory and the Last Judgement when anxious souls asked what they could do to be allowed to see Salvation, the answer was: Believe in Jesus Christ, and do penance, as ordained by the Church. Pray God and his saints for mercy, and do good works yourselves, so as thereby to gain some merit to counter-balance the multitude of your

50

sins. So men strove to lay up a treasure of good deeds. However, the anxious went on asking themselves the same question: Will this be sufficient? Impossible to still the anxiety of the soul. Many asked themselves the same question as Luther: How do I get a Gracious God? It was because it brought the answer to this question that the Reformation was felt as a relief.

THE REFORMATION IN DENMARK

In Denmark, as in other countries, the Reformation was a complicated process, closely bound up with social and political conditions. The co-operation which had been evolved during the late Middle Ages between the higher clergy and the nobility had antagonized peasants and burghers. The Crown was politically and economically interested in putting an end to the Church's concentration of power, while the common people joyfully visualized the possibility of being freed from the heavy tributes to the Church. But the Reformation was also a truly religious popular movement.

The way was prepared for the Reformation by a typical biblical humanism under the leadership of *Poul Helgesen,* a Carmelite monk, who with great energy fought the worldliness and degeneracy of the Church, the sale of indulgences, and the higher clergy's greed for money and power. So he was attracted by the Lutheran movement, but when he realized that it wanted to bring about a breach with the Pope and the Roman Church, he opposed it. Helgesen gives a graphic description of the popular character of the movement. He speaks contemptuously of how "Holy Writ is now being debated publicly at inns, baths, barbers' shops, smithies, mills, customs houses, tradesmen's quarters, and guildhalls, among drunkards and gamblers, dancers and jumpers, by shoemakers, millers, excisemen, and traders . . ."

Already in 1520 *King Christian II,* with the support of townspeople and peasants, tried to introduce certain Church reforms. His aim seems to have been first of all to break the power of the nobles and higher clergy, and to create a National Church, which would keep up the connection with Rome, but of which he would himself be Absolute Head. However, in 1523 he was deposed by the nobles, who put *Frederik I* on the throne. Although the latter had promised to protect and preserve the Catholic Church, the ten years of his reign were marked by a policy of extreme tolerance towards the Lutherans. At first they had their greatest following in South Jutland. Here, with the support of Duke Christian, a Lutheran theological college was set up in the town of Haderslev, and King Frederik even extended his personal protection to some of the Lutheran preachers.

Most important of these preachers was *Hans Tausen,* a monk of the Monastery of St. John of Antvorskov, near Slagelse, in the island of Zealand. After having studied at Wittenberg, he preached for some years at Viborg, where he converted most of the townspeople to Lutheranism. His activities in other parts of the country met with much the same success, and from 1529 Hans Tausen worked in Copenhagen. There his preaching gave rise to a vigorous reform movement, one result of which was an iconoclastic riot in the course of which many valuable works of ecclesiastical art were destroyed.

The representatives of the old Church were able to offer but feeble opposition to the full force of the new popular movement. The connection with Rome was almost broken, and there were not among the Catholic leaders in Denmark men made for martyrdom. At the death of Frederik I, in 1533, the Catholic Church in Denmark was nearing its complete dissolution.

For three years the country was ravaged by a civil war, which was, however, not caused by religious disputes. Victory fell to the above-mentioned South Jutland Duke, who, in 1536, ascended the throne as *Christian III.* In the same year he proclaimed the Reformation. The last Catholic bishops were imprisoned and the Church deprived of its land and, consequently, of its temporal power. The episcopal estates and most other Church land was confiscated by the Crown. A new Constitution was introduced, approved by Luther, and by Bugenhagen, his representative in Denmark. It was based on an entirely new social philosophy: The country was no longer to be ruled by King and Church jointly. The new Constitution laid down that there was but one Authority in the land, the temporal one, to which the Church, too, was subject. But it is, that was made quite plain, a Christian authority, for the King binds himself by solemn promises above all else, to worship Almighty God and protect and maintain His Word.

As leaders of the new Church were appointed nine superintendents (before long, however, the title of bishop came into use again). They were to be elected by the clergy of the towns, but as it happened, the King soon gained the decisive influence on their election. At the consecration of these first superintendents, the Danish Church lost the Apostolic Succession, and there has never afterwards been any wish to re-introduce it.

In the course of the next decades the organization of the new Church was completed. The leading personality in this work was *Peder Palladius,* whose "Book of Visitations" has been preserved and gives a vivid picture of the tangled situation. In 1550 the entire Bible had been printed in Danish (this edition is known as *Christian III's Bible* and is one of the most important achievements of our old Danish literature). In 1569 all the Danish hymns produced during the Reformation were collected in Hans Tommisøn's Hymn Book, admirable more for the quantity than the quality of its contents.

THE AGE OF ORTHODOXY

In the latter half of the 16th century the spontaneous and popular character of the Reformation was lost. For some time Melanchton's view of Christianity (Philippism) exerted a considerable influence in this country. Melanchton stressed the necessity of man's concentrating all his will-power on the effort to believe. The adherents of his view sincerely wished for an understanding with the Calvinists, a tendency which in this country was supported by *Niels Hemmingsen,* a theologian of European fame.

On the other hand, a number of theologians felt obliged to uphold the pure Lutheran doctrine, and this Orthodoxy won the day. Niels Hemmingsen was accused of propagating Calvin's doctrine of Holy Communion and had to give up his professorship, after which, until well into the 18th century, life within the Danish Church bore the stamp of Lutheran orthodoxy. Uniformity was achieved by not tolerating any form of Christianity but pure Lutheranism within the Realm. Only a few provincial towns, e.g. Fredericia, for the sake of Calvinist refugees, such as the French Huguenots, became enclaves of religious freedom. In the long reign of *Christian IV* (1588–1648) the Danish Church was under the firm rule of Bishops *H. P. Resen* and *J. Brochmand.* Undeniably, intolerance and fanaticism are very conspicuous to students of the period. But they did not succeed in drying up the spontaneous expression of piety. From Germany came such devotional books as Johan Arndt's True Christian Faith and Christian Scriver's The Soul's Treasure. At the beginning and end of the period two of our own greatest hymn-writers, *Hans Christensen Sthen* and *Thomas Kingo,* were at work. Especially Kingo's pithy, genuinely Christian hymns, composed in the baroque style, have exerted a never-to-be-forgotten influence on Danish Hymn-writing (p. 8). Through his book of family sermons J. Brochmand was to influence several generations of his countrymen. And several times stern calls to penance swept through the country.

But it was also the age of superstition and witch-hunts. As late as in 1674 a learned headmaster could publish a book on a terrible case of witchcraft practised in Køge.

About the middle of the period, in 1660, Denmark became a hereditary and absolute monarchy. The *Kongeloven* (Law Concerning the Royal Prerogatives) of 1665, however, proclaims as the King's foremost official duty not only himself to worship God as ordered in the Bible and the Augsburg Confession, but also to maintain his subjects in the pure, unadulterated faith as expressed in the Confession, and with his royal power to uphold and protect this faith against heretics, enthusiasts, and blasphemers.

In 1683 was issued the Danish Law, one part of which includes ecclesiastical laws, and in 1685 a new Service Book was introduced.

Thus it was made clear that the Church did not have any kind of independence, but was simply the institution through which the Absolute Monarch ruled the religious affairs of his country.

THE AGE OF PIETISM

The unquestioning faith, which in the Age of Orthodoxy had dominated our entire cultural life, was gradually undermined from several directions. In Denmark, too, was felt the effect of the European revolt against traditional thinking which was the chief aspect of the Renaissance. Traditional ideas began to be replaced by conclusions drawn from experience and experiment. Men began to look for the natural causes of everything. Hence grew a demand for popular education, freedom of religion, and religious toleration. Subjectivism and individualism were proclaimed. Each individual was to find his personal view of life.

Various manifestations of these tendencies are found in two seemingly contrary, but in many respects parallel movements, viz. Pietism and Rationalism.

Pietism made its first appearance in Denmark a quarter of a century after Spener had begun his work. Shortly after 1700 it knocked at our door, pressing its demand that faith bear fruits of good deeds, its methodical doctrine of conversion, its emphasis on Holy Writ as the source and norm of religious life – and its sharp criticism of the state-controlled Christianity of the Church, which, for the purity of its dogma, was inclined to forget that faith is life and should be manifest as such.

In spite of this view there flourished side by side throughout the whole period a Pietism adopted and supported by Church and King, and a revivalism, which was decidedly critical of the Church. Its ideal was the pure congregation, i.e. a group consisting exclusively of converts, or at least awakened, who should be the salt of the dead mass of those who were only Christians by name.

King *Frederik IV* (1699–1730) gave early proofs of his interest in the Pietistic Movement. This interest was due to a mixture of motives, partly an occasional need to do penance for his not very moral life, partly the wish to emphasize his absolute power by securing for himself control of developments, but also partly because he felt genuinely attracted by a form of Christianity which his German-born Queen had adopted whole-heartedly. At any rate, Pietism – in spite of the violent resistance of the orthodox clergy – left many traces throughout his reign. By direct order of the King two young Pietistic priests were called in from Germany in 1705 and sent as missionaries to the Danish colonies in India. Thus Denmark was the first Protestant country to organize a foreign mission. Some years later a *Missions Collegium* (Missions Office) was set up to control it. This office further sent a Norwegian clergyman as a missionary to the Lapps in Finmark, and Hans Egede, an orthodox clergyman, to Greenland. There, amid appalling difficulties and hardships, he rendered highly praiseworthy services as a missionary to the Eskimos.

Under the influence of Pietism a number of philanthropic and educational measures were introduced in the home country. On the royal estates, which were scattered all over the country, the King built two hundred and forty elementary schools. At Copenhagen an orphanage was founded for a hundred poor, parentless children, and its printing-house poured out a stream of religious books and pamphlets. Lastly, an old decree making it compulsory for everyone to go to church on Sundays and holidays, was revived.

At the same time Pietistic groups were formed throughout the country, and especially in South Jutland, which again, as so often has been the case, became the bridge over which spiritual movements passed from Germany into Danish territory. The leaders of some of these groups were clergymen who had joined the movement. Other groups took the form of anti-Church lay conventicles.

The next King, *Christian VI,* (1730–1746) had already as Crown-Prince adopted Pietism. His and his German-born consort's court had been one of the nurseries of the movement. Undoubtedly, he had close connection with separatist circles. Thus he kept up friendly relations with Count Zinzendorff, who, in the early 1730s, visited Copenhagen, and evidently had hopes of considerable possibilities for Moravianism in Denmark. But after his accession to the throne, the King was soon won over to Church-Pietism, which, consequently, was victorious. This gave the movement an advantageous status at the time, but in the long run was detrimental to it. Although the conventicles were not prohibited, many obstacles were laid in their way. The parish priest must be informed in advance of when and where they were to take place, and in case there was more than a very small number of participants, he had to attend them himself. A new decree concerning holidays emphasized the importance of church attendance. In 1736 Confirmation was introduced and with it a very thorough preparatory study of the Christian doctrines, based on a large Pietistic catechism. Finally, a Government Inspectorate was set up, which was to keep the life of the Church under strict control, and soon became an intolerable straight-jacket to it. The small groups lived on here and there, but were unable to achieve anything of importance.

It was left to the hymn-writers of the Pietistic movement to achieve great things. Its greatest hymn-writer was *H. A. Brorson* (1694–1764) (p. 9). He began as parish priest of Tønder, and later became Bishop of Ribe. Not only did he translate considerable numbers of Pietistic hymns from the German language, he also wrote many hymns of his own. Brorson's hymns are still among the living treasures of our hymn-book. He does not entirely eschew the Pietistic tendency to sentiment, which now and again lapses into sentimentality. However, as one of our greatest lyrical poets, he was able, in many of his hymns – often in a graceful rococo style – to find expressions for the pithy, aggressive revivalist tone, and for a subjective fervour which can rise to a pure mystical adoration of Christ.

THE AGE OF ENLIGHTENMENT

The subjective element we find expressed – in an entirely different way in the greatest Danish writer of the Age. This was Professor *Ludvig Holberg* (1689–1754), best known as a writer of comedies. During a long stay in France he was profoundly influenced by Deism and the philosophers of the period of Enlightenment. In his writings, among which are many popular works on philosophy, he criticized our traditional culture, and especially the orthodox dogmas of the Church. Still, Holberg remained fairly moderate, did not allow himself to be carried away into Atheism, but took his stand on a Deism tinged with elements of Christianity, but with the main stress on morality.

This made Holberg the pioneer of those spiritual trends which the Danish Church was to follow in the latter half of the 18th and the opening years of the 19th centuries: the ideas of the Age of Enlightenment and Rationalism. As there are few specifically Danish trends in this development, only a brief sketch of it will be given here.

After the death of Christian VI, Pietism soon lost its hold on the life of the Church and community. The new King and his circle were mainly interested in temporal matters, and the common people breathed more freely now that the spiritual pressure from above had been eased.

For some years after 1750 the predominant idea was a supra-naturalism which had been imported from Germany, and which endeavoured to prove that the Christian revelation was not contrary to Reason, although it does contain elements which transcend Reason. In this country, too, critical voices were heard, but there were few advocates of downright atheism. Historical and critical studies of the Bible and Church History led to a demand for the abolition of such dogmas as were contrary to Reason. Especially in the last decade of the century a more extreme radicalism was noticeable, but on the whole the Danes remained moderate, both in politics and religion. The example of France seemed frightening to most. Instead, much energy was spent on useful social reforms. In 1788 the peasants were freed from the bond-service which had made them little more than slaves of the great landowners. Further, in many ways much earnest work was done for the education of the lower classes. The foundation was laid of a legislation for a country-wide system of elementary schools. Work was started on the education of both peasants and workers. The administration of justice was modified and made less harsh. Jews were given rights of citizenship, and in the colonies the slave-trade was prohibited. The life of the Church was influenced by various shades of rationalism, which all had this in common that there was a greater interest in ethics than in dogmas. Jesus became less the Saviour and Redeemer than an exemplar of the life dedicated to the good of one's neighbour. Many members of the clergy enthusiastically took up extensive work for social reforms. Often they did splendid work, not least in the country parishes, where the parson usually farmed the glebe himself, by leading the way to agricultural reforms. But, from the Christian point of view, it can only be described as a period of weakness.

THE FINAL STRUGGLE WITH RATIONALISM

The structural changes of society which had begun with the important reforms of the late 18th century, were continued and intensified in the 19th century. The influence of what had till then been the ruling classes was reduced in favour of the increasingly influential classes of the farmers, middle-class townspeople, and the workers. About the middle of the century absolute monarchy was replaced by a democratic social system, and towards its close, the country saw a period of general prosperity due to its increasing agricultural and industrial production.

Spiritually, the 19th century is the age of Individualism. Romanticism with its worship of the Genius was continued in Darwin's doctrine of "the survival of the fittest" to reach its climax in Nietzsche's doctrine of the Superman. In Danish literature the cult of the personality was most strikingly expressed by H. Pontoppidan, who in his novel about "Lucky-Per" defines the goal of Man as the will to see himself in divine nakedness, and who thinks himself lucky to have been born in an age which calls for the individuality.

In the life of the Church, too, there is felt throughout the century a tension between the community of the Church and the subjective and individualistic trends.

In the first half of the century the Danish Church bore the stamp of a somewhat conservative rationalism. The public turned its back on the earth-bound utilitarian morality of the Age of Enlightenment, and its superficial optimism which was soon annihilated by the course of political events. The war with Britain in 1807 led to the bombardment of Copenhagen. Another consequence of the war, the British blockade of the Danish seas, brought about the State Bankrupcy of 1813, and the loss of Norway a year later. These events abruptly put an end to the successful economic expansion of the preceding period, plunging the country into dire poverty. In these circumstances, Kant's doctrine of Duty became an important source of inspiration to many Danish rationalists. Nevertheless, as a pointer to where man's duty lay, the Categorical Imperative was less often stressed than the Bible, which was often cited as the source and norm of the Christian Faith. Still, there was no way back to the Orthodox or Pietistic view of the Bible. The critical study of the Bible had raised too many problems for that, and it proved impossible to find a valid solution of this dilemma.

That was to come about in ways which make the 19th century the most extraordinary and interesting in the history of the Danish Church.

Least unusual are the revival movements which, in the first decades, cropped up here and there in the country, some stemming from "awakened circles" which had survived unnoticed from the days of Pietism. Still, a movement which was unlike the others arose in the district between Horsens and Vejle. These "Strong Jutlanders" were inspired by the love of liberty and the dislike of the state-controlled Church. They preached a typically Pietistic kind of penitential piety, penance, and demands for conversion and sanctification, at the same time sticking to the old-fashioned Lutheran doctrine of justification. They only used Kingo's orthodox hymn-book, and the Pietistic catechism, refusing to have anything to do with the successors of these works, introduced in the Age of Enlightenment. For a long time the authorities tried to curb these Jutlanders, but in the end had to give up. At the same time other revival movements, most of them influenced by Pietism and Moravianism, arose in Funen and soon spread to large parts of the country. With these, too, the authorities interfered. Their adherents were fined or put to prison, but increasing numbers realized that the days of State Church regimentation and coercive measures were over. After 1830 there arose in Denmark a rapidly growing Liberal movement, which pressed for freedom, including religious freedom. When, in the 1840s, the authorities demanded, and in a number of cases practised, compulsory baptism of the newborn children of Baptist families, protests were heard from many social groups, including some of the State Church clergy.

This development was partly due to the influence of the English low-church movement. Thus, an English clergyman, working in Copenhagen since 1812, was instrumental in setting up a Bible and Tract Society and a Foreign Mission Society, which was not run by the Church, but by volunteers, supported by congregations influenced by revivalism.

On the other hand, the German influence on the Danish Church was, for once, insignificant. German romanticism and philosophy of nature profoundly affected Danish literature, as also the inspiration drawn from Goethe and Schiller. However, in the first decade of the 19th century only narrow circles of intellectuals were active on that front. Not till somewhat later can Romanticism be said to have affected the mass of the people, and then it mostly took the form of a national revival. It may also be worth noting that Schleiermacher never won a large following in Denmark. With us, the victory over Rationalism was won by a few profoundly original personalities.

Foremost among them stand Grundtvig and Kierkegaard, but mention should also be made of *I. P. Mynster,* parish priest of Church of Our Lady from 1811, and Bishop of Zealand 1834–1854. He came from Pietistic circles, but already in youth had turned his back on them, and had adopted the theological and political radicalism of the Age of Enlightenment. Afterwards the meeting with Kant and German Romanticism made him sceptical of Rationalism, but it was through conversion that he was led personally to accept the Christian

Faith. As a young clergyman he had been convinced by the study of the Bible that, not only had Christ lived and taught as stated in the Gospels, but he was still a living force. This personal experience of Christ as the Saviour determined Mynster's later preaching. Since he was intimately conversant with all sides of the cultural life of the age, his preaching attracted a large section of the cultural elite, and through his written works he influenced still greater numbers. As a spiritual adviser he thought it his paramount duty by means of the Bible to lead each individual to a personal confrontation with Christ. It may seem strange that Mynster, who had preached that religion was a matter for the individual conscience, stressing the fervent acceptance of the mysteries of faith, in his years as Bishop should have become a authoritarian and often obdurate champion of the State Church. It was he who introduced compulsory baptism of Baptist children. The explanation was, however, his conviction that, within the unchangeable frame-work of established doctrines the individual's possibilities of salvation were better protected than within the so-called Free Churches. When what he regarded as a duty to the new-born children was being neglected, the Church was obliged to assume responsibility for them.

GRUNDTVIG'S VIEW OF CHRISTIANITY

Far more important and far more profoundly original was *N. F. S. Grundtvig* (1783–1872). In youth he, too, was a rationalist, secure in his self confidence and conviction of Man's ability to live up to the norms of Christian ethics. This optimistic view of the nature of Man was rudely shattered when, as private tutor at a country house in the island of Langeland (1805–1808), he fell passionately in love with the young mistress of the house. This unquenchable passion opened his eyes to the falsity of the view of human nature which he had hitherto accepted. He discovered in his own heart forces and potentialities too strong for his self-control.

He succeeded in sublimating these forces by concentrating with unparallelled energy upon extensive studies. German idealistic and romantic poetry, which formerly had left him cold, now captivated him as a reflection of a reality in which he had himself lived. He studied Herder, Fichte, Schelling. Above all, he eagerly studied the ancient Nordic myths, finding in them a confirmation of his own newly adopted view of life. The feud of gods and giants was merely the reflection of the eternal struggle between the forces of good and evil in the life which surrounded him. Inspired by Romanticism, he, at the time, thought of Religion as changing forms of the link between the temporal world and Eternity. That is why, in a poem, he called Woden and Christ brothers, both sons of the All-Father.

A couple of years later he himself reacted violently against this denial of the absolute Truth of the Christian Revelation. He took Orders so as to be able to take office as curate to his aged father. He even dreamt of calling believers to wage war on scepticism and rationalism. Then the question struck him with the force of a blow: Are you a Christian yourself? Have your sins been absolved? So he was plunged into a desperate religious crisis, which lasted throughout most of the autumn of 1810, and led to his conversion to a Lutheran and Biblical Christianity. Except for short periods of service as a priest, finally of Our Saviour's in Copenhagen, he lived for the next fifteen years the life of an independent writer, dividing his time between historical studies, especially of ancient and medieval Scandinavia, and the Struggle for the re-introduction of an Orthodox Christianity, firmly rooted in Luther and the Bible. Its core was the conviction that Man is lost without a Saviour, and the foundation of his faith was the Scriptures, God's Revelation to Man which "endureth forever". So he combats both Rationalism and the romantic view of Nature, which, in his opinion, broke down the distinction between the Natural and the Divine, between God and Creation, and consequently between Good and Evil.

His view of the Bible was the fundamentalist one, but more and more he came to feel that he had merely brushed aside the historical criticism of the Bible texts, he had not defeated it. Then, about the middle of the 1820s, he was again plunged into a religious crisis. It was during this crisis that there ripened in him the view which he called his "unique discovery". He published it in 1825, in the course of a controversy with one of the most eminent Rationalists of the day, in the pamphlet entitled *"Kirkens Genmæle"* ("The Church's Reply").

Grundtvig now gives up the Bible as the foundation of faith and sets up the Church in its place, but, be it noted, not the Church as a historic establishment, but the Living Congregation. It is, he emphasizes, older than the Scriptures. Already from the days of the Apostles it has been recognisable, because while pronouncing the Creed it gathered round baptism. Through Holy Communion it received the flesh and blood of Our Lord. When the faithful share the Sacraments, when the words of the Lord at the Last Supper are spoken, and the Creed is recited, then the Lord of the Congregation is present, though invisible. So it is in the Living Congregation that the Christian can at any time meet his Saviour. Some thought they found traces of Catholicism in this. But Grundtvig did not share the Roman Catholic view that the Sacraments work in and by themselves, or through the ordination. They work solely by the Word spoken there, and which has been spoken throughout the whole history of the Congregation. It is a Living Word, for the Lord is Himself present when it is spoken, and fills it with life. Nay, the Word is the Lord Himself. At baptism He makes a covenant with each of us, and through the Lord's Supper the baptized one gets his share of the gifts Christ has purchased with His life, His death, and His resurrection. To Grundtvig being a Christian was not a question of having the right opinions, the right morals, the right religious experiences, but of Christ's intercession to redeem humanity which is lost in sin. Now this intercession takes place only in the Living Congregation when it is united in the cult round the fundamental religious drama. There is, as we have here tried to hint by the use of the words "cult" and "drama", in Grundtvig's conception of Christianity something which points to the fundamental elements of the experience of God as found also in non-Christian religions. However, in Grundtvig it is exclusively concentrated round the Christ who is risen, and lives and works in his Congregation.

This intuition freed Grundtvig from the anxiety caused by the breaches made by biblical criticism in the orthodox view of the Bible.

The Bible as such is not the Word of God. But this does not mean that Grundtvig was contemptuous of the Bible, quite the contrary was the case. Few have lived as intimately with the Bible as he. Its books he regarded as an inexhaustible source of information about God's ways with Man from Creation to Redemption. But by his view of the Church he saved it from falling into the hands of the theologians, the Pharisees of to-day. There will not in Protestantism arise a papacy of the theologians, which was much to be feared, as many would think that the theologians were the best interpreters of the Bible.

Altogether, Grundtvig did not set great store by the office of the priest, and the movement he started, is better described as a low- than a high-church movement. Later this was emphasized by the Grundtvigian formula that the Church is merely a civil institution. This was meant to make it plain that the Organized Church was made by man as a necessary frame for the Christian way of life. In this civil institution the True Church of Christ is staying as a guest.

From 1825 to his death in 1872 Grundtvig was the leader of an ever-increasing following. In 1839 he was appointed chaplain to the Vartov Foundation in Copenhagen, where he worked until his death, for many years as titular Bishop. His views of the Church and Congregation decided the history of the Church and the growth of our national culture. Now we shall point to some of their most important elements.

About 1830 Grundtvig three times visited England, and became an enthusiastic admirer of the spirit of liberty which pervaded the English community, and which, as he thought, had produced remarkable economic and political activities. At home, therefore, he became a tireless advocate of liberty, in the community as well as in the Church. It might have seemed natural for the adherents of Grundtvig to form their own free, living congregations, and some of them did later on. But most of them, like Grundtvig himself, remained within the National Church, fighting for the greatest possible freedom within the given framework. In 1855, the followers of Grundtvig brought about the passage of A Bill Concerning the Release from Parish Ties.

By this new law members of the National Church obtained the freedom to join another congregation than the one they geographically belong to, if the minister of the other congregation is willing to receive them. A later law has permitted the setting up of free congregations within the Church. If at least twenty families wish to do so, they can set up their own congregation and choose their own minister. They can build their own churches, and in several cases have done so, but they can also obtain permission to use the parish church.

Grundtvig's views of the Christian faith and human life find their most forceful expression in his *hymns*. As a writer of hymns he is among the greatest in world literature. He both translated – often with great freedom – German, English, Latin, and Greek hymns, and wrote many of his own. The total number is a couple of thousand, several hundred of which are among the treasures of The Danish Church. No other Danish hymn-writer has equalled the force with which he sang the work of the Holy Ghost in the Congregations – a natural consequence of his conception of the Congregation as the place where the Living God comes to meet Man. But other facets of the Christian faith are expressed in his hymns, too. His intimate knowledge of the Bible profoundly influenced both the hymns and his numerous songs with subjects from biblical history.

Grundtvig was to some extent inspired by Rousseau and the optimism of the Age of Enlightenment. So, contrary to Orthodoxy and Pietism, he emphasizes that the image of God in man has not been erased. To him, Man as created in the image of God, is a mysterious blend of matter and spirit. Its essence eludes rational explanation through precise formulas, be they theological, as in Orthodoxy, or temporal, as in Rationalism. But the truth about Man can be experienced, as it was by Grundtvig, when, on the island of Langeland, infatuation exploded all the theories in which he had until then put his trust. And this insight into Man's true nature can be extended by the study of history and literature. As we have seen, the old Northmen had understood something essential which was expressed in their myths of the war of the good gods and the evil giants. History taught Grundtvig that, whereas the Romans, the

French, and the Germans always have striven to build up a philosophy which would give a complete explanation of human nature, the Jewish, Greek, and English cultures have shown far greater respect for reality: Man is not a machine, a purely rational being, but a creature in whom God through thousands of years of evolution has allowed spirit and matter to clash ("chained spirit and dust together"). In Man there is a vital force which comes from God, and which makes him fundamentally different from the higher animals. The expression of this force is speech, by means of which men alone of all living creatures have been able to find words to express their spiritual life.

To open the eyes of men to such insight is of the greatest importance as a preparation for the words of the Gospel that also this being, in which divine forces are at work, shall be saved – and that no human being, no matter how imbued with the spirit of God, can save himself, that is always Grundtvig's starting point. But from the fundamentals here hinted at he formed the motto which seems scandalous to many: "Be human first, then a Christian". What he wants to say is that first we must experience what it really means to be a human being – must feel the horrors and splendours of life, and realize that throughout life, and in ourselves, too, divine and infernal forces are at war. Only when this has become a reality to us, will we be able to accept the salvation offered us through the Gospel.

It must be added that to Grundtvig man is never an isolated, independent individual, but always a member of the community we call a nation. Every human being's natural speech is the mother tongue, his cultural background is the people's heritage of common memories. All this is a gift from God, and must be respected as a reality. So a man must earnestly endeavour to understand what it means to belong to a nation. In Grundtvig's poetry the religious message is accompanied by descriptions of Danish scenery and of the history of the people. Parallel with all this he explained his ideas of the Christian Faith and the life of man in numerous prose works.

Of course, *education* must have seemed of paramount importance to him. It was to prepare the minds for the acceptance of the Gospel.

So he was not satisfied with schools imparting a merely academic education, even if, of course, such an education was indispensable. The most important task of the school was to give "knowledge of life". Through such subjects as biblical history, mythology, history, and literature the school was to open the eyes of the young to what it means to be a human being, confronted with both the rich potentialities of life and the dangers of error and fall, men should be led to the brink where they are bound to realize their need of salvation, and so to the meeting with God in the Living Congregation. From this meeting they are again forced out into life to work with its endless, God-given possibilities. Such thoughts led, in the latter half of the century, to the foundation of numerous Grundtvigian folk-highschools where especially the sons and daughters of the farms were inspired through a curriculum of history and poetry to undertake their share of the work of building up the newly created democracy. Attempts to contact the young industrial workers of the towns were not very successful. The elementary schools were influenced in many ways by Grundtvig's ideas, even where the teachers did not join the movement. Grundtvig's demand that teachers should tell their pupils the history of their country, etc., read stories and poetry to them, and teach instead of merely ordering them to learn lessons by heart, became a forerunner of valuable elements of the so-called free education, which in the 20th century won the day throughout western Europe.

SØREN KIERKEGAARD

Before giving an outline of the history of the Grundtvigian movement, mention must be made of the other great leader of 19th century spiritual life in Denmark, Søren Kierkegaard (1813–1855).

Søren Kierkegaard's father had begun life as a shepherd-boy on the Jutland heath. Later, as a wool merchant in Copenhagen, he had made a very considerable fortune. He was 56 years old at the birth of his son, had retired from his firm, and devoted all his time to religious ponderings. For he was always burdened with an ineradicable, deeply depressing sense of guilt. His highly gifted son was marked for life by the joyless Pietism of the home, and his father's pathological preoccupation with his own sins. Complying with his father's wish, Kierkegaard took a university degree in theology, but did not afterwards apply for a living. Instead he lived in Copenhagen on his fortune, becoming an independent writer, who in the brief span of his life produced works on theology and philosophy which, for scope and profundity, are unique in world literature. His life was uneventful, but, drawing on his personal experience and vast reading, he produced thoughts which have spread far beyond his day and country. For he delves down to the basic problem of what it is to have *existence*. To Kierkegaard this means more than merely being alive, taking life as it comes to one, occupying oneself with the important or trivial occurrences that meet one unsought, i.e. the life of the ordinary citizen. That sort of thing can be used by men to pass the time, perhaps even to pass it quite sensibly, and usefully, but all the time in dependence of something outside themselves. That sort of life leads to despair, because one is chained to something which, on closer inspection, is found worthless. Now, realizing that one is living in a great void, one is filled with *angst,* indefinite dread. This *angst* is not like fear derived from a definite object, so it cannot, like fear, be overcome by removing the object. *Angst* is the basic tone of one's life, caused by seeing life as emptiness, a void.

To get into the right relationship with life – to win existence – is to assume responsibility for one's conduct of it, i. e. to assume it from the inside as something subjective.

So it is hopeless, nay, dangerous from the outside to set up systems as guides to human life. Since the Renaissance many such systems have been built by men who have not been willing to accept any truths but such as have been derived from experience and logical thinking. Thus they have betrayed the basic idea of Christianity that only through faith can we get in touch with the fundamental and eternal truths. The culmination of such systems, according to Kierkegaard, has been reached by Hegel who, taking as his starting point his famous dialectics, maintains that every phenomenon gives rise to its opposite whereupon the seemingly irreconcilable opposites combine to form a higher unity, thereby producing harmony. The underlying idea is that, by means of his own reason, man is able to arrive at the complete truth about God and the world, leaving no room for the hereafter and Eternity. By setting up the State and its moral organization as the highest, God is reduced from the eternal to the temporal sphere, and the foundation is laid of a dangerous idolatry, the State and life on earth usurping the place of God. So Kierkegaard regarded Hegel as the greatest danger of his day. But he was well aware that we are exposed to the same danger if, on Christian principles, we build systems aiming to give complete explanations, whether, like Orthodoxy and Pietism, we trust that the Word of the Bible is irrefutable, or, like the followers of Grundtvig, we rely on the Sacraments and Baptism, "the little word from the mouth of the Lord". For all such explanations of life Kierkegaard has nothing but contempt. They lead away from the Existential, i.e. our relations to reality, which are not based on logical proofs, but upon each individual's fervently passionate acceptance of the Truth which lies outside himself, and which alone can give direction to his life. In his doctrine of *Stages on Life's Way,* Kierkegaard devotes several books to making a map of existing possibilities. The aesthete relies entirely upon the temporal. The aim of his life is enjoyment, i.e. to draw from life all its tangible possibilities. This may be done through love when, like Kierkegaard's Don Juan-figure, Johannes the Seducer, in "Either – Or", one takes a young girl and enjoys experimenting with her in all the varying phases which lead finally to seduction. It may also be done by regarding health, wealth, honours, or the development of one's own talents as the greatest good, and basing one's whole life on that. However, to many an aesthete Eternity is a possibility underlying his pursuit of worldly pleasures. It can give rise to anxiety, despair, and world-weariness, which can only be overcome by making room for the Eternal.

At the ethical stage, the individual is pressed by the demands of the Eternal, and believes in the possibility of fulfilling these demands in the temporal sphere. To him the purpose of life is work, the faithful discharge of his duties. He does not flit through life, like the aesthete, ever pursuing fresh pleasures. He never tries to avoid repetition. To him the ideal relationship with woman is marriage, by which two beings are ever more and more closely united.

However, through all this man has not really got in touch with the Eternal. That only happens when he acknowledges his guilt. When a man realizes that he has eternal responsibility for his own existence, that, so to speak, he can himself choose – or shirk the choice – then there is born in him a sense of guilt, from which God alone can save him. This is the religious stage. Kierkegaard recognizes two such stages. In the religious stage A man has realized that he is chained to the temporal sphere and cannot himself break away, but, not having entirely given up the idea of his own innate goodness, he recognizes in Jesus Christ the great model. In the religious stage B, on the other hand, man gives up all reserve and takes the plunge into the 70.000 fathoms of the sea, gives up all human security, and accepts Christ as his Saviour. This is a desperate thing to do. To Reason, the idea of Salvation through Christ, is absurd, a paradox. But by the acceptance of this absurdity as his subjective truth a man is led to what Kierkegaard means by an existential relationship to life. Then subjectivity becomes truth. This is not to say that the truth is subjective, and so may be any thing. It means that man gets in touch with eternal truth, which is revealed to him as the Truth – that man fervently accepts a truth which cannot be proved, and which seems absurd, but which is, nevertheless, the only, the vital truth.

It is understandable that a genius struggling with such ideas had to give up the ordinary life of the common citizen. When he had become engaged to a pretty young girl, Kierkegaard soon found that he was not made for marriage, or, in his own philosophical terminology "he was not made to realize the common fate". So he broke off the engagement. For years his thoughts kept circling round this point of his otherwise uneventful life. He kept seeing it in fresh perspectives and drawing fresh conclusions from it.

He was not made for being ridiculed either, as the "Corsaren", a satirical magazine, did when he had recklessly challenged it. During this campaign he withdrew still deeper into his own self. So he came to the conclusion that he who tried to realize eternity in the temporal sphere, must be prepared for mockery, persecution, and martyrdom, as had been the fate of Christ.

Finally, Kierkegaard was not made to serve the Church in the capacity of an ordinary clergyman. He served it in his own way, by holding up to it an ideal, and revealing the distance between the demands of the New Testament and the reality of the Danish State Church. In the last years of his life, he whipped the Church with scorpions, hoping to awaken in some, be it only a very few, the honest will to see how far they were from the ideal, so that they could enter into an existential relationship with the truth and with God. In his struggle to awaken the individual to anxious fervour, Kierkegaard is an exponent of a fundamental 19th century trend. Although he did not become the founder of a movement, his passionate appeal to individual integrity has left deep marks on the spiritual life in Denmark, both within and outside the Church. His warning against setting up false systems has been applied to the collectivistic tendencies of the 20th century. And to-day he has even got followers among the atheists, who, face to face with an existence which seems to them absurd, demand that man take upon himself the responsibility for his own fate, choose for himself, and so enter into an existential relationship with absurdity.

MOVEMENTS WITHIN THE CHURCH SINCE 1849

In 1848 – at the moment when a rebellion in Holstein gave rise to The Three-Years' War with Germany – King Frederik VII gave in to the pressure of Liberalism and promised the nation a free and democratic Constitution.

The Basic Law of the Constitution, which was passed on June 5th 1849, gave the Danes freedom of religion. The State was to be neutral in matters of religion. Nevertheless it was laid down in the Basic Law that "The Evangelical Lutheran Church (i.e. the existing Danish Church) is the Danish National Church, and as such is supported by the State". The reason for this provision is that, in spite of the principle of religious neutrality, the State feels under obligation to support the Church to which the entire nation with the exception of a very low percentage of the population, belongs. Later, when alterations were made in the Basic Law, this provision was preserved. A Church Constitution, which in 1849, it was undoubtedly thought, would be established later, has never come into being. This was largely due to the resistance of the Grundtvigian movement. So, since 1849, Church legislation has been carried out by the secular *Rigsdag* (since 1953: *The Folketing*), administered by a Ministry, headed by a Minister who need not be a member of the National Church.

Another chapter will discuss the changes which have taken place in the relations of Church and State. This chapter will only deal with life within the democratic National Church.

The circles of "awakened" which had been formed in the first half of the 19th century had been absorbed almost entirely by Grundt-vigianism. Many, however, could not accept Grundtvig's view of the Scriptures as "the dead word", and they were also shocked by his positive view of "this world". Some joined the Free Churches and sects which, about the middle of the century, began proselytizing with great energy, e.g. the Baptists and the Mormons. But quite a few did not find a spiritual home until, in the 1850s, a Home Mission Move-ment (Indre Mission) arose, which bore the stamp of Pietism.

Grundtvigianism was the oldest of the movements within the Church, and at first had the largest following. In the course of time, however, it split up into various camps, each emphasizing a different aspect of Grundtvig's manifold activities.

Some emphasized his basic view of Christianity: The presence of Christ in the Living Congregation when it reads the Creed, and when it gathers for baptism or the Lord's Supper. For this section of the Grundtvigians the service and the preaching of the Gospel became the central thing. Grundtvig's words about Liberty and Democracy were harder for them to accept. Politically, this wing of the Grundt-vigian movement was rather Conservative. Other followers of Grundt-vig, on the other hand, stressed his ideas of Liberty and Democracy. In this form, the movement appeared, first of all, to the independent farmers who, after Denmark had been defeated in the war with Ger-many and lost South Jutland, completely reorganized Danish agriculture. While, formerly, it had relied on exports of corn and cattle to Germany, they now concentrated all their energies and intelligence on the production of improved agricultural products such as butter, cheese, eggs, and bacon. A co-operative movement was started, the farmers joined forces to build bacon-factories and dairies all over the country, and start co-operative sales-organisations. In this way they succeeded in creating an important market in Britain for their improved products. The leaders of these vigorous and successful activities were mostly men who had drawn their inspiration from the Grundtvigian folk highschools. They had not there been taught agricultural subjects, but their interest in human and communal life had been stimulated. There is no denying, however, that the preoccupation with such mundane matters tended to swamp the religious aspect which, to Grundtvig, was most essential.

Politically, most of these Grundtvigians joined the Liberal Party (Venstre). This brought them into the company of people whose conception of Liberty and Democracy were not derived from the Gospel, but from European Liberalism, among whose representatives was Georg Brandes, a declared atheist. Many of the older followers of Grundtvig regarded this alliance of "Danish" and "European" Liberalism with scepticism. Even if, politically, it was natural, it was not without dangerous aspects from the point of view of religion. Still more dangerous, perhaps, was the interest taken by the "Leftists" among the Grundtvigians in philosophical Positivism and the critical study of history. The critical study of the Bible did not shock them, for they thought that Grundtvig's emphasis on the Creed and the Sacraments would protect them against the reduction of the value of the Scriptures as historical documents.

By following these and other ways, Grundtvigianism won a numerous following at the cost, some would assert, of a dilution of its ideological content. It was much influenced by Humanism and Liberalism. There have, however, always been those who tried to uphold the original ideas of the movement. In recent years, it has even been possible to speak of a Grundtvig-renaissance. In many congregations, Grundtvigianism is still a living force, and Grundtvig's view of the Sacraments has been of importance to the Danish Church as a whole. Many Grundtvigians have found a salutary cure for the tendencies to dilution in the theology of Karl Barth and a renewed study of Luther.

THE HOME MISSION MOVEMENT

The Home Mission Society, which had been formed in the 1850s, and had absorbed some of the Pietistic revivalists, was reorganized in 1861 as The Church Home Mission Society, whose chairman, until 1901, was a clergyman named Vilhelm Beck.

Before long the Home Mission grew up to be the second important movement within the Church. Its following was mostly recruited among the poor smallholders, farm labourers, and fishermen, and from the lower middle-class townspeople.

In Copenhagen the Home Mission Movement developed along special lines, as will be seen later, but in the country it mostly preached a Pietistic religion of penance with vigorous calls to conversion and sanctification, while drawing a sharp line between believers and unbelievers. Grundtvigianism and the Home Mission not only worked on different social levels, there is also a distinct psychological difference between the two movements. Whereas Grundtvigianism relied on the normal, unbroken spiritual growth of the baptized members of the congregation, the Home Mission stressed the necessity of a sudden conversion, by which the believer purposely turned his back on the "world", taking up the fight for his own sanctification and the salvation of other souls.

Vilhelm Beck was a great organizer. Many clergymen joined the movement, and numerous laymen were employed as book-agents, selling Home Mission tracts, or as missionaries to carry on the work of evangelization in the homes and the mission-houses, which, by and by, were built by the hundred all over the country. Their message was a simple one. Using the Scriptures as the impregnable foundation of their activity, they preached doom and salvation, forcing men to face the questions: Have you found God's mercy? Are you saved?

The possibility of eternal damnation, and the glories of salvation were painted in vivid colours, stressing the necessity of a sanctified life. Socially and morally the Home Mission helped many on their feet, especially among the social outcasts. They found a home in the meeting-house, in the midst of those who shared their faith. Thus they were snatched away from the evils of drinking, gambling, and immorality, and given a new self-respect through their efforts to bring others to salvation. The extent to which the Home Mission Movement succeeded in realizing Luther's conception of the universal priesthood is most impressive: he who had received the light must – both by word and deed – proclaim his salvation. The work of evangelization was not only kept up in this country, the movement also took up the Foreign Mission. Through the Danish Mission Society and other new organizations missionaries were sent to non-Christian countries. Everywhere tireless efforts were being made to save souls from perdition.

The force of this movement was largely due to its narrowness. It was difficult for its adherents to accept other types of Christians. The Grundtvigians were mostly regarded as "wordlings", and biblical criticism was the doings of Satan. They turned their backs on the cultural life of the nation. Only one thing mattered: salvation or damnation. So the Home Mission Movement did not exert any direct political influence. The social problems, whose solution became increasingly urgent with the rapid expansion of the community, met with little interest in most Home Mission circles. Many were narrow-minded, and the isolation in which their small groups lived, tended to foster priggishness and Pharisaism.

On principle the movement must needs be extremely critical of the National Church and its members who were baptized, it is true, but Christians in name only. – It would, therefore, have been natural for the Home Mission to secede and start a Free Church, using the meeting-houses as churches. But this did not happen, and it remained a Church Home Mission Society. The most important reason for this may have been the part played by some of the clergymen of the National Church as leaders of the movement. Moreover, Grundtvig's doctrines of the importance of the Sacraments may also have served to keep them within the church. Be that as it may, in spite of its critical attitude to "unbelieving priests", the Home Mission stayed within the Church, considering it their duty to act as its salt.

In Copenhagen, the Home Mission developed along different lines. In the latter half of the 19th century, the city rapidly expanded beyond its ancient walls and moats. New industries sprang up, extensive working-class quarters spread round the old city, a stony desert made up of blocks of cheap small flats into which too many inhabitants were crowded. This gave rise to enormous social problems. So industrialization was followed by the Socialist struggle for higher wages, shorter hours, and better housing. Few of the clergy understood what was happening, usually they sided with the "haves" against the "have-nots". So the Socialists were driven to regard the Church as an enemy and a servant of Capitalism. The fact that the work of building new churches in the capital had come to a standstill did not improve matters. There were parishes of as many as 70.000 inhabitants. Under such conditions, the all too few clergymen had no chance to get in touch with their parishioners.

Then the Copenhagen Home Mission began its work. While, in the provinces, the movement concentrated exclusively on evangelization, its adherents in Copenhagen – as also in the German Home Mission – were aware of the necessity of making philanthropic efforts to relieve the extreme distress of the poor. At the turn of the century the Copenhagen Church Fund began to collect money for the erection of new churches. The aim was to create parishes of 10.000 inhabitants. The following chapter will describe these efforts (page 35, 107, 150), and the social and philanthropic aspects of the work. Suffice it to say, at present, that the antagonism between the Labour Movement and the Church has been almost entirely overcome. It has, however, been impossible to prevent the mass of the population from sinking into an attitude of passivity to the Church of which, nevertheless, the great majority remains members.

Besides Grundtvigianism and the Home Mission, the National Church has been influenced by a *third movement*, representing a mediatory broad-church view. The work was begun by Mynster and H. L. Martensen, his successor and, since 1899, the movement has been organized as the "Kirkeligt Centrum" (Church Centre Party). – It has endeavoured to gather all Christians round the Church and its divine service, in sharp contrast to the tendency of the other movements to isolate the faithful in "Living Congregations", or in the societies organized by the Home Mission round the meeting-houses. The "Kirkeligt Centrum" has never won a large following, but to many of the clergy it has been a spiritual home. Here was openness to both theological and social problems, and a keen interest in the adaptation of the Gospel to the demands of a new epoch, both as regards evangelization and education. This movement has attracted persons of widely different theological opinions, Conservatives as well as Liberals.

In the years immediately preceding World War I *the liberal theology* came to the fore. Its attempts to reconcile the Gospel and modern philosophical and scientific studies gave rise to a trend in evangelization which was widely felt both in Grundtvigian and Home Mission circles, especially in the Y.M.C.A. and Y.W.C.A., which had been started by the Home Mission, and in the Christian Student Movement. While keeping up the revivalist tradition, those who were influenced by liberal theology would often hold up Jesus as the ideal who appealed to the best in human nature.

One of the leaders of the movement was Olfert Ricard (1872-1929) a parish priest who was secretary of the Copenhagen Y.M.C.A. 1896-1908 and, besides, for sometime secretary-general of the Y.M.C.A. in Denmark. Through his writings and speeches he greatly influenced the work among the young. Churches were packed when he was the preacher.

In the 1920s a violent reaction set in against this humanization of the Gospel. A group of theologians gathered round a magazine called *"Tidehverv"* (The Era). They were inspired by Kierkegaard and the early Karl Barth, and afterwards more profoundly by Bultmann. So they have maintained that not only the liberal theologians, but the Grundtvigians, too, have betrayed the Gospel. In contradiction to the belief that the Christian religion was the road to security and happiness on earth, they have proclaimed the absolute nothingness before God of all that is human. They have endeavoured to purge the doctrine of all social elements, and to proclaim the scandalous and anti-human nature of the Gospel. He who comes up against the Gospel's condemnation of human nature has but one thing to do: to accept God's forgiveness and go out into life and carry out his earthly duties.

In the 1930s many Danes were caught up in the *Oxford Group Movement,* which arranged several large-scale campaigns in this country. In recent years this movement, reorganized as Moral Re-Armament, has been active in Denmark, but has only very slightly affected the life of the Church.

On the other hand, a *High-Church Movement* has been able to win a following in the post-World War II years, and has stirred up heated discussions. Its spokesmen assert that the loosening hold of the Church on the people is due to the fact that, in the course of time, its divine service has become diluted and impoverished. Theologically they represent a kind of Neo-Orthodoxy. They revive some of the elements of medieval liturgy which had not been rejected by the Reformation, but which had since fallen into disuse. In this way they aim at making the church service richer than is usual within the National Church. Consequently, they have been accused of wishing to lead the Danish Church back to Rome.

So there are several conflicting views within the Danish Church. None of the old movements has escaped the influence of the modern trends. The greatest effect has been produced by the criticism of the *"Tidehverv" Circle.*

There is, nevertheless, no denying that the majority of the Danish people take little interest in the Church. Most babies are baptized soon after birth, and funerals without the services of a clergyman are rare, but between these two extremes, large sections of the population have only sporadic contacts with the church. This is the Church's greatest problem-to-day when it is so well provided for by the modern welfare state.

AN EVANGELICAL-LUTHERAN CHURCH

Clause 3 of the Basic Law of the Kingdom of Denmark, of June 5th 1849, reads as follows: "The Evangelical-Lutheran Church is the Danish National Church". As the Basic Law defines our National Church as "an Evangelical-Lutheran Church", it may be useful to consider what that means.

That it is possible to speak of an Evangelical-Lutheran Church at all is a piece of historical irony. For Luther had no intention of establishing a new Church. On the contrary, he asked that no Church be called by his name. The first time we meet the word "Lutheran" is when Johannes Eck uses it in one of his books as a term of abuse.

Luther set himself the task of being a "voice" within the existing Church, a voice calling for a reformation based on the new insight into the nature of the Gospel. Luther intended to lift up his voice within the walls of the Church, and true Lutheranism must acknowledge this intention. However, the Lutherans gradually formed a religious community on a par with the Catholic Church and the Orthodox Churches. Its status as such was already formally recognized by the Augsburg peace treaty of 1555, which put an end to the religious war. Its first clause was to the effect that Catholicism and the Catholic Empire were still the foundation of Germany, but in the special circumstances the Catholics recognized the right of the Lutherans and their Church to exist within the Empire. The equality of the two Churches was finally established in 1648 by the peace of Westphalia. The schism was now complete.

The special doctrines of Lutheranism were developed through a dispute on two fronts. In his quarrel with Catholicism, Luther mainly worked out his doctrine of justification by faith and of the Christian's freedom. On the other hand, his campaign against "enthusiasts" led to his doctrine of the authority of the Scriptures. For, in the opinion of these enthusiasts, any authority was evil, served only to prevent the work of the Spirit. So they rejected Luther's doctrine of the authority of the Word, because it came to them from outside, instead relying on what they called "the inner light". They also rejected infant baptism, besides the sacraments and other "outward things" which seemed to them inessential. Against these two adversaries, Catholicism and the enthusiasts, Lutheranism has ever since had to witness.

Lutheran Christianity has two basic dogmas: the authority of the Word of God, and the justification by faith.

To Luther, the *Word of God* is first of all Christ, *the Word* (John 1.1 *et seqq.*). Through Christ, God speaks to and works with Man. He did so once, when Christ was here on earth, and He still does so to-day, for Christ speaks to Man through the Church. Lutherans are firmly convinced that, whenever the Gospel is preached as He ordained, Christ, true to his promise, is Himself spiritually present and speaks His Word to men. To Luther, the Word of God is a *spoken word*. But the source and norm of this spoken word is what the apostles spoke of Christ, as recorded in *the Bible*. By its witness must all sermons, nay, all that takes place in the Church always be judged and, if necessary, reformed.

In Lutheranism justification by faith is not a dogma among many others. It is the very essence. Its starting point is a new conception of what the Bible means by the Justice of God. Intensive studies of the biblical texts convinced Luther that justice is not a quality which is given to man, or which he acquires, but that a man is justified when God has mercy upon him and, for Jesus' sake, forgives his sins. This basic conception colours the Lutheran view of all that the Christian has and is. Faith, Hope, charity, sanctification, etc., all are gifts that come to him *from outside*. These two basic dogmas unite in what Lutheranism calls *the Evangel*. It is the joyful tidings that Man's iniquities are pardoned undeservedly for the sake of Jesus Christ, by faith. And this Evangel comes to us in several forms. It comes by word of mouth, both when it is preached publicly from the pulpit, and individually when, *at confession,* the priest promises us forgiveness of our sins. Further, it meets us in *baptism*, which is God's promise of forgiveness of all our sins, a promise which is valid throughout our lives. And it meets us in *the Lord's Supper,* where we receive the Body and Blood of Christ "given and poured out for us for the forgiveness of our sins".

When this has been said, we have accounted for the essence of the Lutheran view of the Church. The Church lives and is nourished by the Word of God, says Luther. In its article about the Church, the Augsburg Confession says that it is "the congregation of the sanctified, in which the pure Gospel in preached, and the Sacraments are administered rightly". It is characteristic of the Lutheran Church that it has considered evangelization and the Sacraments equally important. It must be added, as a characteristic feature of worship within the Danish Church that, in this Lutheran Church, the Sacraments have been given a position of unique eminence.

It is characteristic of the Lutheran Reformation that, in giving rules for the outward life of the Church, it was very conservative. Only such parts of the ritual as were openly contrary to the Gospel were abolished. Thus, f. inst., the Danish Church has preserved the chasuble, while other Lutheran Churches, influenced by the Reformed Church, have abolished it. Also, Luther was very loath to give his opinion of the kind of Constitution which the Church ought to have, or of the relations between Church and State.

This conservatism has been very pronounced in Denmark. Perhaps too much so, for it has also influenced dogma. The Reformation was completed throughout the country by Royal Decree, but that did not prevent a certain "Reform-Catholicism" from living on and affecting popular piety to this day.

So the Danish Church cannot be said to have clear-cut dogmas, and frequently movements of various kinds have tended to swamp its specific Lutheran message.

Such was the Evangelical-Lutheran Church for which, after three centuries of evolution, the makers of our free, democratic Constitution had to assume responsibility. Its basic doctrine had been shaped already in the century of the Reformation, when the entire Danish nation adopted the Lutheran faith. However, this basic doctrine was not explicitly stated until 1683, in the Danish Law. In its section "On Religion" it says: That religion shall alone be permitted in the King's realms and lands which is consonant with the Holy Bible, the Apostolic, Nicene, and Athanasian Creeds, the unaltered Augsburg Confession, received in 1530, and Luther's Short Catechism". So the word of God as revealed in the Scriptures, the three symbols of the Ancient Church, and, as specific Lutheran features the Augsburg Confession and Luther's Short Catechism, are the foundation stones of the Danish National Church. Reference is made to these foundation stones in the vow, which Danish clergymen sign at ordination. It reads as follows: "I, *NN,* who have been lawfully appointed to a living, and who, in my conscience, know that I have not used any dishonest means to obtain this appointment, promise before the face of Omniscient God: First: that I will be studious to preach the Gospel pure and unadulterated, as found in prophetic and apostolic Scriptures and in the symbolic books of our Danish Evangelical-Lutheran National Church; with all due reverence to administer the Holy Sacraments as instituted by Christ, and, in so doing, as also in performing the other sacred functions, to perform everything in accordance with the ordinances of the National Church.

Further: That, to the best of my ability, I will hinder the abuse of the holy means of grace, and oppose such doctrines as are contrary to the Creed of the National Church, as also that I will work diligently on the Christian instruction and education of the young.

And lastly: that I will endeavour by diligent and earnest study of the Word of God and the holy doctrines of religion ever more to perfect and render myself more capable of performing the duties of this holy office, and endeavour, as a minister of the Word should, to be a good example to the congregation, as also, in the performance of all my various duties with all due compliance to obey the ecclesiastical laws and ordinances, and to behave to my superiors and colleagues in such a way as not to give cause for complaint. All this I promise, while remembering the day of reckoning, conscientiously to keep, as God gives me grace to do so."

That is: the Danish National Church preserves its Lutheran foundation by recognizing Luther's Short Catechism and the Augsburg Confession as its basic documents.

It will be remembered that the Augsburg Confession was formulated by Melanchton and his assistants at the Diet of Augsburg, in 1530, to give the Emperor a favourable impression of the religious views of the Evangelicals. When it was shown to Luther — after it had been submitted to the Emperor — he thought that it was too accommodating to the Catholics, but did not want to alter it. This Confession is now included among the symbolic books of nearly every Lutheran Church. The Danish Church recognizes it as one of its symbolic books from a conviction that, in essentials, it accords with Holy Writ. To us it is a guide to the correct interpretation of the core of the Scriptures — not a conclusive document containing infallible dogmas. Theoretically a new insight, derived from a profounder understanding of the Scriptures, could lead to an alteration of the Confession.

Similarly, Luther's Short Catechism has been regarded not only as a statement of the basic teachings of the Evangelical-Lutheran religion, but as the Church's guide to the meaning of the biblical message.

It is, of course, obvious that this basically Lutheran view has been adapted by the Danish National Church in its own independent way. This is true of its organisation, for a description of which readers are referred to a subsequent chapter, and it is equally true in the ecclestical and theological spheres, where, as we have seen, sacramental doctrines have played a characteristic part. They have, for instance, been the stabilizing element in 19th century revival movements within the Danish Church.

To this Danish National Church, which is Evangelical, the vast majority of the Danish people, presumably about 95 per cent of the population, still belongs.

Until the passing of the Basic Law in 1849, the Evangelical-Lutheran Church was the *State Church* of Denmark. Membership of this church was compulsory for the King's subjects, with the sole

84

exceptions of a few Calvinists and Jews. The King was Absolute Ruler of the Church as of all other functions of the State. But by the *Kongeloven* (Law Concerning the Royal Prerogatives) the King was bound to the Augsburg Confession, and obliged, in the phrase of the day, to keep his subjects to the only true religion.

The Basic Law gave the country freedom of religion. Not only was the freedom of the individual guaranteed, so that his civic and political rights were in no way affected by his religion. Danish citizens could freely form sects and denominations to worship God according to the dictates of their consciences.

Consequently, there are in Denmark besides the National Church a number of denominations, some of which have received Government recognition. These *recognized denominations* can, on certain conditions, obtain Government authorization of their ministers. By this recognition, which does not in any way detract from a non-recognized sect's freedom to form a congregation, the ministers of the denomination are authorized to perform clerical offices (baptisms, weddings) with validity before the law, and so to keep church registers. Government recognition also gives the members of a denomination certain advantages as regards taxation.

Recognition of a denomination will depend of its numbers, the permanence of its organization, and its ability to recruit and train ministers, so that its continued existence and supply of ministers are guaranteed.

There are at present 9 recognized communities, among others the Reformed Church, The Roman Catholic Church, and the Mosaic Community.

THE DANISH NATIONAL CHURCH

"The Evangelical-Lutheran Church is the Danish National Church, and as such supported by the State." This is the full text of clause 3 of the Danish Basic Law.

The preceding chapter has made clear what it means that the Danish National Church is Evangelical-Lutheran. This chapter is to explain in what sense this Evangelical-Lutheran Church is a National Church, and not as, before 1849, a State Church. We shall also examine its organization.

The Basic Law did not make all religious denominations equal. Since almost the entire population belonged to the Evangelical-Lutheran Church, the former State Church was given a special position.

It was the intention to give this Church a position of greater independence of the State than that of the State Church, yet, at the same time, to link it more intimately with the State than all other denominations.

What was to be the position of this Church, the rules regulating its connection with the State, the Basic Law did not say. The solution of this problem was postponed. It was to be solved later by the Legislature. Clause 80 (later clause 73) of the Basic Law reads as follows: *"the organization of the National Church is to be made the subject of legislation"*.

No doubt, at the beginning, the Fathers of the Constitution had in mind that, by the introduction of some kind of representative synod, the National Church should obtain some degree of independence of the Government. However, in spite of the repeated attempts in the course of time, of various Church-Commissions and Committees, it has been impossible to agree on such a Church Constitution. This failure to fulfil the promise of the Basic Law is partly due to the unwillingness of the Folketing (Parliament) to give up its monopoly of Church Legislation. The Folketing does not in this, or in any other respect, wish to see its legislative power supplemented by similar representative bodies. Partly, it was due to the inability of the Church to agree upon a Church Constitution Bill. Some of the causes of this inability to reach an agreement can be listed: 1. Originally there was among the clergy a certain anxiety lest the laity should gain too much influence over the government of the Church. 2. A considerable wing of the Grundtvigians, who wanted the congregations to grow independently, feared that a Church Constitution would be a hindrance. In the Grundtvigian view "the Church is a civil institution", which was to provide the soil for the free growth of the Living Congregation. So they were content that the Church should be controlled by the non-denominational Parliament and the politico-juridical Government. 3. The revivalist sections of the Church were afraid that non-Church elements, not "the Living Congregation", should gain control of a representative Church Assembly. Lastly, certain Free Church groups regarded the complete separation of Church and State as the ultimate goal.

The separation of Church and State, has, of course, been repeatedly ventilated both by the supporters of the Church and by the politicians. At present, however, this problem can hardly be said to be of topical interest.

Consequently, the central government of the Church has remained in the hands of the same bodies which control the affairs of the State. The legislative power is vested in the King and Folketing (Parliament), and the work of administration has been carried out by a politically elected Minister, who need not be a member of the Church. Formerly the *Kultusministerium* controlled both Church and Education. Since 1916, the administration of the Church is the business of a special Church Ministry.

The lack of agreement on the constitution of the Church has not prevented the Legislature from passing a number of important Church bills, *e.g.* the *Act Concerning the Release from Parish Ties* (1855), which gave the members of the Church the right to have sacred functions performed by a priest of their own choice instead of the local parish priest. *"The parochial tie"* is an expression used to describe the fact that, before 1855, a parishioner was tied to his parish church and parish priest, and had no right to have sacred functions performed in other churches or by other priests. There was also the *Law Concerning Electoral Congregations (1873),* which made it possible for a smaller circle within a parish to constitute a congregation and elect its own priest. So the *electoral congregations* are free congregations within the Church. They defray all expenses themselves: pay the priest and sacristan, and have their own board of governors. Their priests are ordained by a bishop, must have a letter of presentation, and sacred functions performed by them are legally valid. They have the right to use the parish church, and are subject to the rules of ecclesiastical inspection, but their ties with the National Church are less formal. Lastly, we must mention. The *Law Concerning Access to Clerical Office* (1947), which gave women the right to apply for clerical offices within the National Church.

This law gave rise to considerable dissension within the National Church, the effects of which are still felt, even if only one of the country's ten bishops still refuses to confer holy orders on women. Primarily, this was, of course, a quarrel about whether the Church had the right to confer holy orders on women. However, the underlying question, which to many was far more important, was that of the State's right through legislation to interfere with what must be regarded as "internal Church policy". True, the Folketing might, with some degree of truth, be said not to interfere. It did not settle the question of whether a congregation or the Church in general was to have women as priests. It merely allowed women to apply for clerical offices, leaving it to the Church to decide whether it would employ them.*)

It is arguable that neither the Basic Law nor later legislation can be used to support this distinction between "internal" and "external" affairs, of which only the latter should be within the province of the Legislature.

However, wide circles within the Church were of opinion that, on

*) At the moment ten women are priests within the Danish Church.

The mansion of the Bishop of Copenhagen facing *Vor Frue Kirke* (The Church of Our Lady).

The Church Ministry is housed in the same building as the Ministry of Education.

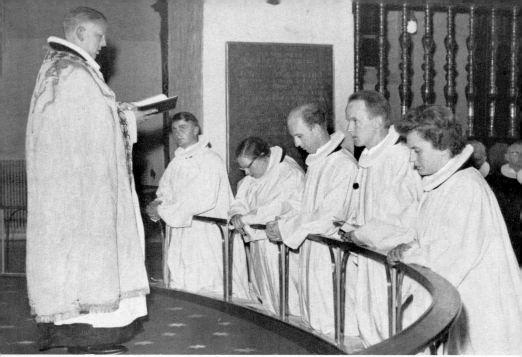

Ordination at Elsinore Cathedral.   *Next page.* Ordination at Roskilde Cathedral.

At the consecration of churches the Sacred vessels are carried to the new church by a procession of priests; this is equally true of the church housed in a barrack as of the large brick church.

Kalbak Church in the Faroes.

Below. Klaksvig Church in the Faroes.

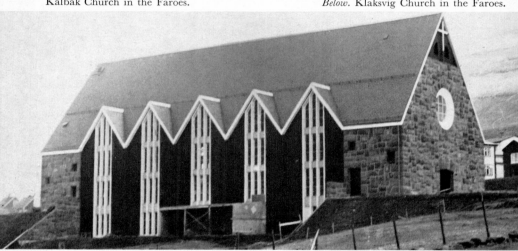

The church of Sukkertoppen, Greenland.

this occasion, the Folketing had not adhered to the traditional considerateness with which it has usually handled the affairs of the Church. And this change of attitude was made in spite of the fact that the Folketing had to reckon with a very unfavourable reception for the bill by a large majority of the members of the representative Parochial Church Councils.

PAROCHIAL CHURCH COUNCILS

This brings us to the mention of the most important of the entire body of Church Laws, *The Law Concerning Parochial Church Councils,* which in its original form dates from 1903. At the same time we shall be describing the units of which the Danish National Church is made up.

The Rules Concerning Membership of the National Church, which, because of the freedom of religion granted by the Basic Law, had become fairly complicated, are laid down in the said law as follows:

Members of the National Church are:

1) persons baptized in the National Church.

2) persons baptized in an Evangelical-Lutheran community other than the National Church, who have later joined a congregation within it. Those who were baptized outside the Realm, become members at their taking up residence in this country, unless they have, in the manner prescribed by the law, made known their wish to remain outside the National Church.

3) Other persons, who have been adopted into some Christian Church by baptism, and who, either through the decision of the

been brought up in the faith of the National Church, or at a later age personally have joined a congregation within the National Church.

The membership is terminated when a member:

1) terminates it by a written declaration, as prescribed by the law,

2) joins a denomination outside the National Church; or when in some other way, such as by re-baptism, he dissociates himself from it.

Next the law expounds the regulations of Parochial Church Councils.

Each parish*) must have one (or in some cases more than one) Parochial Church Council. Members of these councils are: the permanently appointed priests of the congregation and 6–15 elected members according to the population of the parish. Members are elected for a period of four years. At their first meeting they make a solemn written declaration of their intention conscientiously to carry out the duties with which they have been entrusted, in loyalty to the Evangelical-Lutheran National Church, so that it can offer a good soil for the life and growth of the Christian community. However, the law makes it clear that the duties of the council are mainly administrative. In the conduct of his office the priest is independent of the congregational council.

Among the council's administrative duties are the management of churches, graveyards and lands, control of ecclesiastical coffers, appointments and discharges of church-servants, except those who, as civil servants, are appointed by the Church Ministry.

Further, the Parochial Church Council has a voice in the introduction of new hymnals, changes of liturgy and ritual, and the introduction of newly authorized books for the confirmation classes or the religious instruction of the elementary schools.

Finally, the Parochial Church Councils take an active part in the appointment of priests and election of bishops.

It must in fairness be added that, in many parishes, the Parochial Church Councils make large and important contributions both to evangelization and the welfare work of the Church, and that the Parochial Church Council often becomes a useful forum for discussions of the affairs of the parish and congregation.

---

*) The Danish National Church has 2313 churches, and the number of parishes is roughly the same. The populations of the parishes vary from 111 inhabitants in the smallest to over 22.000 in the largest one.

For the elections of Parochial Church Councils the various parties within the Church (the revival movements, Grundtvigians, and Ecclesiastical Centre) are of some importance. One of the political parties, too, has nominated its own candidates. However, in their capacity of members of the Parochial Church Councils, the majority of those elected have considered themselves independent of political and church parties.

There is no official connecting link between the Parochial Church Councils but for practical purposes regional associations and a *National Society of Parochial Church Councillors* have been formed. Here, members gather for an annual meeting when problems of common interest are discussed.

THE PRIESTS

The priesthood is open to persons who have graduated with a degree in theology from one of the two Danish universities. Both the universities of Copenhagen and Aarhus have divinity schools. They do not aim at a denominational training, but provide a free scholarly course in theology, normally lasting 5 or 6 years.

Further, the priesthood is open to missionaries of the Foreign Mission who, after having passed a special university examination, have seen at least seven years' service in the mission fields, and to priests who have, for at least seven years, served Danish Evangelical-Lutheran congregations outside the Kingdom. In special cases, the priesthood can be made accessible by Royal Decree to others, e.g. persons who have a university degree other than that in divinity.

Lastly, a Parochial Church Council can obtain permission to have appointed as priest a person who, without having been trained in any of the ways specified above, through his work for the Church and congregation has been found qualified for the priesthood.

Besides the already mentioned university course the priests-to-be have to take a six months' course at the Copenhagen pastoral seminary, which is affiliated with Copenhagen University, but has its own Board of Governors, of which the Bishop of Copenhagen is Chairman. This course includes homiletic, liturgy, and pastoral theology, while at the same time the candidates serve a Copenhagen parish where they are given an opportunity to preach and get familiar with the life of a congregation.

Before ordination by the bishop of the diocese, the candidates for the priesthood undergo a "bishop's examination", which is less a test of their knowledge than an informative interview about the problems of the priesthood.

At ordination the candidates make the vow already cited in the preceding chapter.

Before a priest can enter into his living, he must have *"collation"*, *i.e.* a formal letter of presentation, whereby the bishop of the diocese, hands over the ecclesiastical office to an ordained person. This letter of presentation is read at the service.

The King appoints all permanent priests, on nomination by the Church Ministry. This Ministry advertises all vacancies. Applicants send their applications to the Parochial Church Council through the Church Ministry. Guided by the bishop, the council then makes the nomination. If it is unanimous it must be followed by the candidate's appointment by the Ministry. So the influence of the Councils on the appointments is very considerable. If, however, the nomination is not unanimous, the Church Minister is free to present any of the applicants for appointment by the King.

In the discharge of his official duties the priest is independent of the Parochial Church Council.

The National Church at present has 1824 priests in active service, of whom 1366 are parish priests. – Besides priests, town churches have parish clerks (who do the office-work and assist in the services), sacristans, and organists.

DEANS

The dean is the local controlling authority in clerical affairs.*) He is chosen from among the parish priests of the deanery, nominated by the Church Minister, who beforehand seeks the advice of the bishop of the diocese, and appointed by the King. The dean of the cathedral

*) The Church has 99 deaneries.

of the diocese is also diocesan dean, i.e. deputy for the bishop during vacancies in the bishopric, or in the absence of the bishop.

The deans deputize for the bishop and see that "everything is carried on decently and properly everywhere".

Among the duties of the dean are 1) as chairman of *the Select Committee of the Deanery,* which besides himself has two lay members elected by the Parochial Church councillors of the deanery, he controls the economy and administration of the parsonages, livings, churches, and graveyards. 2) He inspects the parish registers kept by priests, parish clerks, and village schoolmasters, with the respective archives.*) 3) He inducts the clergy of the deanery.

BISHOPS

At the head of each diocese**) there is a bishop, who is the highest local authority in clerical matters.

When a bishopric falls vacant all members of the Parochial Church councils are given the opportunity to vote for the candidate whom they wish to have appointed as bishop.

The Church Ministry asks the councils to submit the names of the candidates, and sends out ballot-papers. If, at this poll, a candidate has obtained two thirds of all votes, he *must* be nominated for appointment by the King. If none of the candidates has obtained a two-thirds majority, it is up to the Ministry to chose one of the candidates for appointment by the King. So far, however, the candidate who obtained the majority has always been appointed.

The Danish Law***) imposes upon the bishop the duty of teaching others Holy Writ, of preaching the word of God to the

---

*) From time immemorial the National Church keeps *parish registers,* which contain records of sacred functions, and a register of civil matters (births, etc.)

**) The country is divided up into 10 dioceses, to which must be added that the Faroes, which belong to Copenhagen Diocese, have their own Suffragan Bishop.

***) King Christian V's Danish Law of 1683, which still to some extent regulates the life of the Danish Church.

people, not only in the town of his residence, throughout the whole diocese, wherever he goes. Besides, through frequent visitations the bishop is to see that the priests dutifully preach the Word of God.

To this must be added a number of administrative duties. With the diocesan prefect he constitutes the *Diocesan Authority*. This authority administrates the capitals of the churches and livings, and inspects the church buildings. The bishop is the intermediary between the Church Ministry and subordinate ecclesiastical authorities. He provides substitutes during vacancies, dedicates churches, gives permissions to changes of the usual hours of the Church services and to minor changes of liturgy. As chairman of nomination meetings of the parochial church councils and advisor concerning the qualifications of applicants, the bishop takes part in nominations for office. He ordains priests and issues letters of presentation to livings within the diocese.

Once a year, in each diocese, a so-called *"landemode"* (diocesan meeting) is held, which is attended by the bishop, diocesan prefect, and all the deans of the diocese. An inaugural service is held, in the course of which newly appointed deans are installed in office. After the service, negotiations take place about the business of the diocese.

The diocesan meeting can be expanded by invitations to the clergy and parochial church councillors of the diocese.

Besides all this, the bishops are the advisors in ecclesiastical matters both of the Church Ministry and of the subordinate clergy.

In matters of general principle, the Ministry quite frequently takes the advice of the *College of Bishops,* which meets twice a year. The Ministry then asks the Bishop of Copenhagen to put the matter before one of the frequent *Bishops' meetings.* Seing that these meetings are not authorized by law, they may be regarded as "private". To Copenhagen Diocese belong the *Faroes and Greenland.*

In 1963, however, the Faroes were given their own Suffragan Bishop with extensive powers.

The Faroes, whose total population is less than 35.000 are divided up in 11 clerical districts *(præstegæld)* with 17 priests. There are, however, 57 churches in the Faroes, and, travelling between the islands being so difficult, the priest can only hold service in one church within his district. So in all the other churches of the district there is a so-called *"degnegudstjeneste"*. From among themselves every parish has elected a layman (schoolmaster, merchant, or fisherman) to be their parish-clerk *(degn)*, who in the absence of the parish priest conducts the church service consisting of hymn-singing, liturgy, and a sermon, which he reads.

These services meet with the active and enthusiastic participation of the parishioners, and offer an interesting manifestation of the universal Christian priesthood. Altogether, the laity is very active in the life of the Faroese Church, *e.g.* in the wide-spread Seamen's Mission.

Everywhere in the Faroes the people are enthusiastic church-goers, and the congregations have kept up their old-time piety.

The *church-language* is almost everywhere the Faroe language, there being at present only one Danish priest working in the islands. Both the Old and New Testaments have been translated into Faroese and authorized by the King in 1961 and 1937 respectively. In 1960 the Hymnal of the Faroe People was published. While speaking of hymns, mention should be made of the special Kingo-tradition*), which in remote districts has been of great importance both for the Church and the people, but which in our modern age is sinking into oblivion.

The Faroe priests are trained at the Danish universities.

The Faroes are the only part of the Danish Realm to have a considerable growth of *Free Churches*. Thus, about the middle of the last century, the Plymouth Brethren gained a foothold on the islands, where they were called Baptists. They reject every kind of church organization, the priesthood, and infant baptism, but gather round the Scriptures and exegesis, sing hymns, improvise free prayers, and practise meditation.

Especially, on the northern islands, they have gained a considerable following.

---

*) A national treasury of hymn tunes to which the hymns of the Danish 17th century poet Thomas Kingo have been set.

Greenland's population, after an explosive growth in this century, is now a little over 34.000. The last decade has seen radical changes of the social structure, which are bound to influence the Church, too. Before 1950, Greenland was a closed country, and all influences on the people under control. To-day technical expansion, urbanization, and manifold outside influences on the religious life, too, are now pouring in on the population. In many respects, all this has produced a noticeable restlessness.

In Greenland, more than anywhere else in the Danish territories, the National Church is still the stabilizing factor, beloved by the Greenland people. In Greenland the church service is a popular festive occasion, where the living tradition of the National Church is kept up in the families, the children's, young and old people's community gathered round the Word and Sacraments.

The Greenland Church has 18 clerical districts with 22 priests. To assist them in the performance of their duties throughout these enormous districts they have 174 first class catechists, catechists, and schoolmasters, who besides teaching school in their settlements, are also employed as unordained, clerical assistants.

These catechists, all Greenlanders (Eskimos), usually have a Greenland teaching diploma. The value of their work within the Greenland community can hardly be over-estimated, they are closely in touch with the people, its guides in more than religious matters.

Most of the 22 priests are Greenlanders and only a few of them have undergone a theological training, corresponding to that of a Danish priest. Often, by many year's experience as catechists, they have proved themselves suitable for the ministry, and so have been ordained.

Two or three are Danes, who, after acquiring their university degrees in theology and taking special courses in the Greenland language, have been sent out. For the services are conducted in the Greenland language, the majority of the people having very little knowledge of Danish.

Even more than the hymn singing of the Faroe people, that of the Greenlanders is wonderful to listen to for the outsider who attends a church service there. The congregation obviously loves singing the hymns, and has a considerable gift for part-singing. So the Greenland hymn-book is a valuable asset. The Old and New Testaments have both been translated long ago, but the Greenland translation is soon to be subjected to a needful revision.

So far, congregations in Greenland have had no representative bodies, but recent legislation has introduced representation of the congregations, but not with as extensive powers as the Danish parochial church councils.

The administrative head of the clergy is the Dean of Greenland, who, on behalf of the Bishop of Copenhagen, dedicates churches and ordains priests.

The administration of the Church of Greenland is in the hands of the Ministry for Greenland.

CONCLUSION

Presumably this chapter will have made it clear to the reader that many problems of the relations between the Danish National Church and the State are still awaiting their solution. We have a Church without a Constitution, with a secular Parliament as its legislative and financial authority*), and a political Minister as its highest administrative authority. By many this is regarded as an intolerable arrange-

---

*) Until well into this century the *Church was economically self-supporting.* Expenses for salaries, repairs of churches, etc. were defrayed out of its own means (income from real property, land, capital, etc.). Rising expenditure and, perhaps even more, changing financial conditions and legislation, made considerable inroads in the capital of the Church. So now only a small fraction of Church expenditure is paid with the Church's own money. Most of it is paid by Government grants and through taxation of the Church membership. This Church tax is assessed simultaneously with the assessment of other rates and taxes.

For the financial year 1960–1961 income was as follows:

Rent of land, interest on capitals, etc. about .... kr. 11.000.000
Government Grant .... about .... kr. 40.000.000
Church tax .... about .... kr. 97.200.000

Total about .... kr. 148.600.000

ment, which leaves the Church with a minimum of independent authority, and, consequently, driving force. In their view the label says "National Church", but what it really covers is a State Church. It is felt that the days of this arrangement must be numbered, it is a relic of the age of Constantine, unsuitable to modern conditions.

However, whether this prophesy be true or not, and whether or not the view is correct that the separation of Church and State would give the former more "drive", there are, within the Danish National Church, considerable numbers who hold that, by and large, this vague position of the Church has provided a useable frame for its work. Even if, of course, in the current of life, it will be found wanting in some respects, it has always proved strangely able to give scope for a working Church and a free and active congregation.

CHURCH ACTIVITIES

"My stay in Denmark has taught me to value my own religion", a young Moslim from the Middle East told me one day. He added, "For I found out how little the Christian religion means to you Danes. So I, who had never before had any sense of obligation to my religion, of course had to consider whether I, too, could do without my religion".

Such a remark is rather startling. It is, however, not an isolated example; others have got the same impression of Danish Church-life. People all over the world have been informed that Denmark is an ancient Christian country, and that almost the entire population (95 per cent) belong to the National Church. But visitors to the country did not feel that the Church played a very important part in the lives of the Danes. There were of course numerous fine churches, but if one entered to attend the service, they were often shockingly empty. And a meeting with Danes would often make one feel like the Moslim. Or like the American who, when interviewed by a newspaper, said "I have been very surprised every time I asked young Danes about religion and God to find that they blushed and turned away in embarrassment".

Is this, then, the truth about the Danish church? Well, it is part of the truth. The relatively small number of those who take part regularly in the life of the Church is sadly disproportionate to the large number of Danes, who, through baptism have got their home and citizenship within the Church. As *Kaj Munk* the priest and play-wright, once said: Everybody wants to believe in God, but also, by all means, to avoid exaggeration.

However, this is not the whole truth. For it is not just that the churches are there, and the church-bells hospitably invite men and women to come to their services. The Church not only meets the majority of its large membership on the great occasions in their lives. It also endeavours both to invite many children, adolescents and adults to hear *the Word,* and to be of material assistance to those who need help. The Danish Church carries on its work among our fellow-countrymen in foreign parts, and, lastly, it is engaged in Foreign Missions and in the ecumenical work.

It may not be at all easy for a visitor to find out about this day-to-day work of the Church. We know from experience that the disproportion of the large membership of the Church to the few who attend its services, is far more conspicuous. So it is all the more needful and pleasurable here to give a short account of the daily work of the Danish Church.

THE SACRED FUNCTIONS

Confirmation. The great majority of Danish boys and girls (about 93–94 per cent) attend confirmation classes for about six months, after which, at a festival service one Sunday, they are confirmed, not – as f. inst. in the Roman-Catholic and Anglican Churches – by a bishop, but by the priest whose classes they have attended.

It is to be hoped that already before they began school, the children have been taught by their parents to fold their hands in prayer, just as, for seven or eight years, they have been given the religious instruction at school which is the presupposition for infant baptism. But while at school the emphasis is on the imparting of knowledge, the young in the confirmation class meet the Christian religion as something which concerns them far more intimately – as an invitation to share the Christian faith and the life of the Church.

Formerly, it was the custom for the confirmands themselves to answer "yes" to the three parts of the Creed. Now it is more usual for the children to speak the Creed in chorus, or for the priest to pronounce it on their behalf. Next, the priest mentions each confirmand by name, with the laying-on of hands and says: *Almighty God, who has formerly by holy baptism accepted thee for His child and made thee heir to the Life Eternal, may He keep thee in this the grace of thy baptism until thy last hour. May he grant thee steadfastness in thy faith, for the salvation of thy soul.*

One of the first Sundays after the confirmation, quite a number of the confirmands come to Holy Communion for the first time. Unfortunately, for some it may also be the last time – at least for years. In this connection it should be mentioned that, in the Danish Church, children are no less welcome at the Communion-table than adults.

What does confirmation give the young: Not always what was aimed at in the preparations for this sacred function. At least, *Hans Christian Andersen,* perhaps Denmark's most famous son, told us in his memoirs how, as he was standing in the Cathedral on the day of his confirmation, he would constantly think of his boots, the first pair he had ever owned. "My joy at possessing these boots was overwhelming. My only fear was that not everybody should see that I was wearing boots, so I pulled up the tops to cover my trouser legs, and thus accoutred strode up the nave. My boots squeaked, a sound which filled my soul with joy, for it would tell the congregation that my boots were new. But my pious mood had evaporated. I realized this and, with terrible pangs of conscience, became aware that my thoughts were just as much with my boots as with the good God. From the bottom of my heart I begged His forgiveness – and afterwards went on thinking of my boots."

To-day, too, many confirmands have similar experiences. Their minds are full of their new clothes, the anticipation of gifts, etc. But does the sacred function make any impression on them, at all? Quite possibly there may here be cause for concern. But it should not be forgotten that, in the course of many lessons, these young people have been confronted with the Christian faith, a store of the Word of God has been deposited in their minds, and, at the confirmation service, God's blessing sounded in their ears.

What if some of the young do not want to attend confirmation classes and be confirmed? It is for themselves and their families to decide. But in some places – and especially in the large towns – a youth festival is arranged for them. This has sometimes been called a *civil confirmation,* but as there is nothing to confirm, this name is quite

101

misleading. It is, on the other hand, only fair that these young people should not be deprived of a festivity on the threshold between childhood and adolescence.

Marriages. It is a far smaller number of Danes (about 80 per cent) who come to the Church for their weddings. If the couple who are planning their future together, have no regular contact with the church in their daily lives, it may seem right for them to go to the burgomaster for a civil wedding. Still we agree with these words from one of the sermons of Kaj Munk: "Young women are nearly always charming – but most charming as brides. Not those who go before the registrar in the town hall. They are not proper brides, just contracting parties. What a drab and cheap age is ours, to cheat a young woman out of becoming a bride. Cheat her out of church, and organ-music, the white wedding dress, the veil and myrtles and, worst of all, the outstretched hand of God."

Nevertheless, there are still considerable numbers who, on this decisive day of their lives, seek the house of God. – After a wedding hymn has been sung, and after a short address by the priest, the couple standing before the altar are asked as follows: *"Will you, N.N., take* (here the name of the other party is mentioned), *who is standing beside you, for your lawful wife (husband)?"* The groom or bride answers *"Yes"*. *"Will you love and honour her (him) and live with her (him) both in good and bad times, whatever fortune Almighty God has ordained for you, as a husband (wife) should live with his lawful wife (her lawful husband) till death you do part?"* Again the answer is *"Yes"*. To confirm their pact the couple now join hands, and the priest places his hand on theirs saying, *"Inasmuch as you have formerly exchanged solemn promises to live with each other in marriage, and have now publicly confirmed these promises before God and before us, who are here assembled, and clasped each others hands in confirmation thereof, I now proclaim you as lawful husband and wife before God and men."*

The Church demands promises of everlasting fidelity, not only as long as the prospects are bright and promising, but also through the difficulties of everyday life.

If, nevertheless, the couple later on apply for a divorce, then – to prevent them from taking rash steps in so important a matter – it is laid down in the law that an attempt at mediation must be made by a priest. (In case both parties wish to do so, they can apply to the civil authorities for mediation).

While, f. inst., the Roman-Catholic Church in no circumstances permits divorce, it is the rule of the Danish Church that, in case a divorced person wishes to enter into a new marriage, this can take place in a church. Nevertheless, individual priests are free to refuse to assist; after which the person in question can apply to another priest.

Funerals. At a meeting of a group of workers, which took place in a Danish deanery the relations between individuals and the Church were being discussed. No doubt, quite a few of those present were not in very close touch with the Church. Then some one said, "Well, now we have got civil baptism (naming); we can obtain civil confirmation and civil marriages; and we can get civil funerals. But does any of you believe that we can obtain a civil resurrection. What if it stopped at death?" More or less consciously, no doubt this thought, and our total helplessness in the face of death, lead the majority, in spite of all secularization, to arrange funerals from churches or cemetery chapels, with the assistance of a clergyman, for their departed (about 95 per cent).

Curiously enough, the Danish Church has no fixed rituals for burial services. As a rule 2–3 hymns are sung, some words from the Holy Scriptures are read, and the priest makes a speech – often including some words in memory of the deceased.

Afterwards the coffin is carried into the churchyard and lowered into the grave. Now the priest steps up to the open grave, saying: *"Praise be to the God and Father of our Lord Jesus Christ, who in his mercy gave us new birth into a living hope by the resurrection of Jesus Christ from the dead."* Then he throws three spadefuls of earth down upon the coffin, saying: *"Dust thou art, to dust returnest, and from the dust thou shalt again arise."* Finally, the priest says the Lord's Prayer, and pronounces the blessing.

In recent years, and especially in the towns — *cremation* has become customary. At first, the Church was opposed to this innovation, but to-day hardly anybody would attach importance to the way in which the burial is carried out.

The numbers here mentioned concerning the sacred functions of the church are the averages for the whole country. There is, however, a great difference between the circumstances in Copenhagen, in the large provincial towns and in the country. About half of all the weddings in Copenhagen *e.g.* are civil marriages. Later on such a wedding – if the two parts involved want it – may be blessed by the church.

THE PARISH

The Priest and the Parsonage. One of those who, in spite of the obvious disproportion of the large membership of the National Church and the small minority who take part in the life of the Church, saw something very promising in the Danish National Church was a priest named *Morten Pontoppidan.* In his memoirs, he tells how one Sunday when he was pronouncing the aronitic blessing in front of the altar, "I took courage and gave myself up to an urge ... to let my heart go out to all indiscriminately – to pour out the blessing upon all those who had come to church, and also to those who had not come, but still belonged to the parish, whether or not they could be reckoned as members of the so-called "Living Congregation"."

This attitude to the parish and all its baptized inhabitants undoubtedly reveals both goodness of heart and Christian charity. However, that does not mean that everything is as it should be. No, all the members of the Church should be happy in their membership and find inspiration in it to live in the presence of God.

So most Danish priests carry on from day to day an earnest and

104

purposeful work to persuade as many as possible to come and hear the Word of God, and share in the life of the Church.

How is this work done? In many different ways, of course. Not only can the parishioners freely come to their parson, if they want to talk over their problems with someone, or are in need of spiritual guidance. Further, the priest often goes the round of his parish to visit the inhabitants at home, especially, if news has reached him that someone is ill. Many priests organize Bible-readings here and there in the parish, and in many parishes the parsonage hospitably opens its doors to various groups, *e.g.* Bible-classes, and study-groups, mission-groups, and meetings of the old people of the parish, on which occasions coffee is consumed by the gallon! Formerly, the parsonage used to be the cultural centre of the parish. To-day the Lutheran parsonage could be better described as an important force in the clerical work of the parish. In many parishes, the parson's wife deserves a special chapter, for she is the indispensable supporter of the work.

Two Houses. In many Danish parishes we find two houses of a special kind. As a rule they are neither very large nor imposing. Frequently, they are not beautiful either, having been erected at a time when there was a shortage both of money and of good taste.

One is known as the *Assembly-House,* and was built by the Grundtvigians. A group, mostly of young people who had gone to a folk highschool and been inspired with an urge to start a new life, founded lecture-societies, youth-clubs, physical training clubs, etc. All these would often expand to such an extent that there was not sufficient room for them in the homes or in a school-room. Soon an *Assembly-House* would be built, and before long they would spread far and wide in the parishes that were influenced by the Grundtvigian movement.

The other house which is commonly found in a Danish parish, is known as the *Mission House.* It owes its existence to the other great Danish revival movement the *Home Mission* (Indre Mission). It is entirely different from the first one. People came to the Grundtvigian Assembly-House, not only to hear the Word of God, but also for physical training, amateur theatricals, and festive evenings with music and dancing, and were alive to the possibilities of human life, national culture, and the lessons of history. In the Mission House, on the other hand, were spoken earnest and rousing words about the frailty of human nature, sin and guilt, but also about the grace and forgiveness of God, and the Heavenly Home. Many have gone home from the Mission House with peace of mind, renewal of their strength to live this difficult human life, and an ardent wish to draw others also to the Kingdom of Heaven.

The people who flock to the two houses, belong to the same nation and the same Church. Nevertheless, especially in former days, they have had considerable difficulty in understanding each other. It was hardly possible for those who belonged to one house to set foot in the other. Now the differences are less marked, and in parishes where the two inspiring movements spread, the inhabitants to-day seem, more than their forbears, to be aware of the true meaning of the word *neighbourliness*.

As we have already said, the two houses – as opposed to the parish church – are not ornamental to the landscape. But each of them has had its special and very important contribution to make to the Church life of the parish. For from them laymen – mostly in co-operation with the parish priest, who usually felt at home only in one of the houses – have carried on energetic activities including gatherings and meetings for the young or elderly. Often too the houses have opened their doors to evening-highschools and youth clubs, to housewives' clubs and meetings for newly-weds, Sunday schools, and various other activities.

The activities centered upon and radiating from the assembly houses and mission houses now seem to have culminated. But the two houses are still standing, and are still characteristic features of the Danish parish.

The Sunday service and the daily work in all the parishes is what matters most for the life of the Danish Church. It rarely gives rise to sensational news, but as *Søren Kierkegaard* said, "It is not what is noisiest at the moment that matters, but what echoes through Eternity".

Not only are many of the less formal church-activities in the parishes parts of a larger whole; but through the independent church organizations and institutions – of which we have many in Denmark – the Church also endeavours to get in touch with people who may not feel at home in the congregation. This is especially true of the Capital and of the larger provincial towns, whose parishes do not, as in the country, form an organic whole.

In all these independent activities which aim at calling the indifferent to church special mention must be made of the endeavours of the laity.

Before the granting of the Constitution of 1849, preaching the Gospel was the clergy's monopoly. Indeed, there have been times when laymen who gathered friends and neighbours in their homes to read the Bible or expound the Word, were dragged before a judge. Now the situation is quite different. Many of the laity, men and women, are engaged in the work of the Church. This is most fortunate, firstly because it makes our Church a true Folk-Church, secondly because, under modern conditions, the clergy could not possibly cope with all the work unaided, and thirdly because many problems can best be solved by the co-operation of priest and layman.

The Copenhagen Church Fund. "The Church shall be every man's home", says an old Danish law-book. However, a necessary prerequisite is a sufficiency of churches. And it simply was not available in Copenhagen at the close of the last century.

During the period of industrial expansion the population of our capital city had risen from 135.000 (in 1850) to 475.000 (in 1900). To-day it has long since passed the million. While the capital was well provided with schools, banks, cinemas, etc., no provision was made for new churches. Consequently, the old parishes soon became unreasonably large – the population of some exceeded 50.000. So, of course, the contact between church and parishioners became correspondingly tenuous.

Fortunately, there were some who could not calmly witness this fatal development. About seventy-five years ago a group of Church-people-laymen and clergy realized that it would be most disastrous for the country as a whole if Copenhagen became the city without churches. So they started The Copenhagen Church Fund (Det københavnske Kirkefond). Voluntary contributions from all parts of the country provided the necessary means, and soon so many churches were built all over Copenhagen that those years have rightly been called the second great period of church-building in the history of Denmark, the first being the early Middle Ages.

By its efforts The Copenhagen Church Fund has made a unique contribution to Danish Church life. It began as a protest against the Government's neglect of urgent demands for new churches. However, once the churches had been built, they were, so to speak, at once accepted by the Government. The necessary divisions of parishes were made, and the new churches were made to function in exactly the same way as the old parish churches.

Recent years have seen excellent co-operation of Government and Church Fund. The collection of funds is no longer the main purpose. For, contrary to what was formerly the case, the Government is now prepared to make relatively large contributions to the building of new churches. And, by the way, The Church Fund's efforts are no longer concentrated on central Copenhagen, but on the large, hastily expanding suburban municipalities.

However, for the building of new churches the initiative and perseverance of The Church Fund are still indispensable.

THE WORK AMONG CHILDREN AND ADULTS

The Sunday School plays an important part in Danish Church activities. "There is no need to show a child the heavens", says a pagan proverb. However, even if children accept the Gospel more readily than adults, the church has a special duty to the little ones. Admittedly, it is primarily the task of the parents and school to tell the children of the Christian religion, but some special work among them is needful, seeing that there is so much to draw them in the opposite direction. Besides, both parents and school may fail the child in this respect.

This is where the Church comes in with its special children's services and Sunday schools. There are now in Denmark more than 1500 Sunday schools with 6.000–7.000 voluntary teachers (both men and women) who, Sunday after Sunday, devote their time and strength to an effort to help the children – in their way – to remember the Sabbath, and to share the life of the Church.

Infant welfare centres and parish kindergartens.

While the inspiration for the Sunday School work came to us from the west, the inspiration for the infant welfare centres and kindergartens was drawn from the south, or grew out of our native soil.

The need for infant welfare work was felt, because, in the years 1901–05, one out of every six babies died in its first year of life – an infant mortality rate which was almost unparallelled in Europe. So The Copenhagen Association of Parochial Social Services (De samvirkende Menighedsplejer, vide p. 161) set up six infant welfare centres in the church halls of six Copenhagen parishes. Here, mothers could come with their babies, have them examined by a qualified doctor, themselves be taught baby-craft, and besides get a litre of milk. Nowadays there are more than 30 such child welfare centres closely connected with the churches of Copenhagen, and infant mortality has dropped to only one death in the first year of life per 21 babies. Evidently the public authorities must have been following this enterprise with great interest, for when they, about ten years ago, appointed health visitors in Copenhagen, the latter were given instructions to work in close cooperation with the church health centres.

The history of *the parish kindergartens,* of which there are many both in Copenhagen and in the larger provincial towns, goes back to the time of World War I. There was, in those days, a Christian doctor who – shocked by the terrible housing shortage and the overcrowded and unhealthy small flats, he had himself seen when going his daily rounds, and by the miserable conditions under which the infants had to live – started a campaign to relieve the distress. He pressed home to the Church its absolute responsibility for these baptized infants, and called upon it to bring relief. Soon the first primitive kindergartens were set up in the church halls. Afterwards, one parish kindergarten was opened after another, and many of them to-day are housed in well-equipped localities which come up to the highest hygienic and educational standards.

The Y.M.C.A. and Y.W.C.A. "If ever Satan should suffer an injury which would really scorch his skin, it must be through young people growing up in the knowledge of God", said *Martin Luther,* the father of the doctrine of the Danish Church.

However, it was not until rather late in the 19th century that the Church really "discovered" the young, and began to take special care of them.

True, we know that *Ansgar,* the missionary who brought Christianity to Denmark, worked for the young. He even bought some boys and set up a school for them to "train them for the service of God". It is also a fact that *Peder Palladius,* the first Lutheran bishop of Zealand, when on episcopal visitations, spoke many good and forceful words to the young. Nevertheless it was only a little more than 80 years ago that the Church – again inspired by the English example – started an all-out campaign among the young, aiming to lead them to conversion and faith and to an active and spiritual life in God. (Before that there were only the Grundtvigian Youth Organizations *vide* p. 145).

The impulse for the *Young Men's Christian Association* and the *Young Women's Christian Association* came from abroad. But these associations of the young, whose great leader was *Olfert Ricard,* are not mere importations, but also the legitimate offspring of the Home Mission. Of course this double origin is still noticeable in the youth movement. It has always kept a window open to the wide world, been keen to learn and receive impulses from abroad, and has eagerly taken part in international co-operation and intercourse. On the other hand, the youth movement has never been so deeply absorbed by internationalism as to forget that it is primarily a Danish movement, started by, and still affiliated with, the Home Mission and the Danish Church.

At present these associations which own large buildings in many towns, have more than 100.000 members.

Their aim is still "to lead the young to Christ". Formerly they concentrated their rather one-sided efforts on large meetings, and Bible study circles. Nowadays, while still remaining true to evangelization as their primary purpose, they have launched manifold and varied activities, such as study-circles, debating-clubs, sports clubs, choirs, orchestras, boarding houses, etc. The youth movement has also taken up certain kinds of welfare work, started a publishing house, and publishes several magazines.

In the course of the last decades this youth movement has worked more purposefully for the Church, realizing that it is not enough to gather the young in an association. The youth movement must work tirelessly to make the young feel at home in the congregation, at the church service, and at the Communion table.

The Uniformed Corps. Experience has taught us that there are many to whom the above-mentioned youth movement did not appeal. Some might join an association for a short time, only to drift away again, others did not reply to invitations at all. This set some leaders of the youth movement thinking. They saw that, to get in touch with certain types of young people, they would have to appeal first of all to their energy and sense of responsibility. These were to be canalized into athletics, marching trips, manual work, "good-turns", camping, etc. And they were to participate in an active fellowship, where their energies would find a healthy outlet. Not that the Christian element was to be reduced. It was still to be the primary consideration. But, seeing that many were unwilling to be mere "listeners" to Bible-lessons or lectures, it was essential to meet them on their own ground, and try new methods.

These considerations led – under English influence – to the foundation of the *Y.M.C.A. Boy Scouts,* the *Y.W.C.A. Girl Guides,* and the *Boys' Voluntary Corps,* which was modelled on the *Scottish Boys' Brigade.*

These uniformed corps soon became immensely popular, and, contrary to the "civilian" movements, are still expanding.

"We come from the *Church,* where we have prayed God to bless the King and his men. We might also have come from the woods and fields, where we camp in God's open country. Or from the gymnasium, where we go in for physical training. All this we do in the hope of training young men and women for the service of our country and our nation". This is an approximate rendering of words spoken at a parade in the presence of the King. They state in so many words that these uniformed corps are part of the Danish Christian Youth Movement.

THE DANISH ASSOCIATIONS FOR THE YOUNG

About a score of years before the seed of the Y.M.C.A. and the Y.W.C.A. was laid in Denmark, Grundtvig and his disciples had won a large following among the young people of Denmark. They were able not only to inspire them with renewed, patriotism and cultural life, but also to guide the young to Christ. About the turn of the century, some of these disciples of Grundtvig founded *the Danish Youth Organizations* (De danske Ungdomsforeninger), which have now grown into a nation-wide organization, with a membership of approximately 50.000.

As a natural consequence of the Grundtvigian love of liberty, the leaders of these associations have not wished to tie their activities down to a rigid programme. So the local branches can organize themselves and set about the work as they choose. Also they have eschewed employing too direct propaganda methods in their endeavour to bring the young to conversion and the life in Christ. It is hoped that the spiritual life of the individual will develop in accordance with the law of Nature. Then, in God's hour, it will blossom into faith. To an outside onlooker, the "national" element sometimes seems to dominate the work of these associations. However, their laws state their aim with sufficient clarity: *It is the aim of the association to work for concord and fellowship among the young, as also, through patriotic and Christian education, to guide them towards the goal: a keen, Danish, Christian Youth.*

Undergraduates and pupils of the gymnasiums. In close co-operation with *The World Student Christian Federation, The Christian Student Movement of Denmark* carries on a mission among the undergraduates of our two university towns of Copenhagen and Aarhus. This student movement is not affiliated with any church party; it wants all undergraduates to feel at home within it throughout the years which for their studies they have to spend away from home.

The Christian Student Movement has sometimes been referred to as "the Balkans of the National Church" – because of the constant unrest within it – and not without reason. Undergraduates, also Christian ones, are a turbulent race, fond of heated discussions and warfare, and unafraid of discords and ruptures. Undergraduates "are young, and they are being trained to question and to criticize. This can go too far, but basically it is a sign of energy and intelligence which is often combined with a marked sense of the genuine and the consequent receptiveness". (*N. H. Søe*).

Would not it be better if the undergraduate shared the ordinary Christian youth movement? Are they too intelligent to join the Y.M.C.A. and the Y.W.C.A.? These questions have sometimes been asked. However, undergraduates have special problems of their own, and special ways of solving them. So they need a special forum, where they can meet in a Christian academic society for lectures, discussions, and fellowship, and face the traditional motto of the student movement: *Sursum Corda!* Lift up your hearts!

Working in close contact with the Student Christian Movement, *the Christian Movement for the Pupils of the Gymnasiums* (Den kristelige gymnasiastbevægelse) energetically and courageously tries to gain a foothold in all Danish *gymnasiums* (secondary schools). Much of the work is carried on by very young undergraduates, and is, especially in these years when so much Christian work among the young is at a standstill, a model of vigour and enthusiasm. The best way of getting in touch with the boys and girls of our gymnasiums is to invite them for some days to a camp.

The Student Circle (Studenterkredsen) carries on its Grundtvigian activities in academic circles, trying to establish contacts between the undergraduates and the work carried on at the time among the Danish people, trying to summon the young to face the manifold political, cultural, and spiritual problems of the age.

Soldiers. There is another category of young citizens who, like most undergraduates, have to spend a period of time away from home and their usual associates, *i.e.* those who are going through their National Service. With the approval of the military authorities, work has been started there too. Many *Soldiers' Homes* have been opened. The hosts of these homes are prepared to act as advisers in both mundane and spiritual matters of the conscript from the day he has to put his civilian clothes into storage. Some of the soldiers' homes, which are usually situated just outside the barracks, are run by *the Grundtvigian Soldiers' Mission,* others by the *Y.M.C.A. Soldiers' Mission,* and others again by *the Dannevirke Society.* Here soldiers or marines can take coffee, read their home-town's newspapers, take a nap, write letters to their mothers – or girlfriends, talk to their comrades, and lastly get a chance to listen to lectures and Bible-classes. In many soldiers' homes the last items of the evening's programme are hymn singing and short prayers.

Many have, after their National service, told us that, while they were "wearing the King's clothes", the soldiers' home was their refuge in leisure hours.

The Danish Folk-Highschool. Anyone who is even superficially acquainted with Danish Church history, must again and again have come upon the name of *Grundtvig.* His view of life underlies the laws guaranteeing the freedom of worship which are characteristic of the Danish Church. His hymns are part of nearly every church service. He it was, too, who advocated the Danish folk-highschool, which is probably the most characteristic feature of Danish popular education.

While freedom within the Church is almost inexplicable to other nations – even the Swedes don't quite understand it – and while only a few of Grundtvig's beautiful hymns have been translated into foreign tongues, the folk-highschools have influenced education in countries far beyond our boundaries. This school for young people between the ages of 18 and 25 soon turned out to be an excellent export article. To-day folk-highschools modelled on the Danish ones are to be found in many countries.

It was, however, not Grundtvig himself who realized his idea of a folk-highschool. He was the inspiring originator of the idea, but left it to *Kr. Kold,* Denmark's only pedagogic genius, to realize his ideas. It was he who found the method of imparting to the young through lectures, and by vividly telling them of Scandinavian mythology, history, and literature, a conception of all aspects, good or bad, of our national life. Grundtvig had spoken of "the living word". Kold used it in his teaching, thereby helping the young to attain "faith in God's love and in Denmark's happy future".

For nearly a century, the Danish folk-highschool, where about one in ten young Danes has spent six months of his life, has been "the soul of Danish activities within a wide section of the people, in religious, national, and practical matters".

The idea of the folk-highschool has been adopted by other than Grundtvigian circles – both outside the Church (The Workers' Highschools) and inside it. Thus the *Home Mission* owns a number of successful highschools, which, by and large, are run on the same lines as the Grundtvigian ones, except that they apply themselves more directly to evangelization. For, while the Grundtvigian slogan is: "Be human first, then a Christian", the Home Mission highschools change it to: "Be a Christian first, then human".

The above-mentioned folk-highschools – to which the imparting of specific knowledge, which can be put to vocational use, (let alone examinations), is a secondary consideration – have provided the inspiration for quite a few agricultural schools, Nurses' schools, and schools for adolescents (aged 15–17), continuation schools, evening schools, etc. To some extent all these are similar to the folk-high-schools. They provide the same free life as their pupils would have lived at a "real" highschool, while at the same time stressing the vocational and utilitarian aspects of the curriculum.

A school of a special kind is the *Danish Bible School* which provides many short courses, correspondence courses too, in order to help the participants to attain to a clearer and profounder understanding of the Bible text and the biblical world.

The Young Homes' and Laymen's Foreign Mission Movements. In the book on Christian Ethics which most theological students in Denmark study, the above-mentioned Professor *N. H. Søe* says: "Every Christian is called upon to serve, not only in the sense of regarding his daily work as an act of worship, which he sanctifies by the Word of God and by prayer, but also by passing on the Gospel . . . Christianity is mission, and every Christian is called upon to be a missionary, a witness, a messenger".

Many of the Danish laity have understood these words, and known how to live up to them. This we hope to have made sufficiently clear in what we have already recorded. Many other instances of the enterprising and zealous spirit of the Church might deserve mention, but we shall limit the number to two: *The Young Homes* and *Laymen's Foreign Mission Movements* (L.Y.M.).

The Young Homes Movement, which is a recent innovation, grew up because it was found that many of the young couples who, before their marriage, used to take part in the Christian youth movement, after they had married, had difficulty in finding a way to share the life of the Church. They were tied down by household work and children, and they found the usual church circles anything but interesting.

Then some one got the idea of inviting these young people to special meetings and conferences, which, in lectures and discussions from a Christian point of view, dealt with such subjects as the daily life of the married couple after the first fine raptures of love have evaporated, home-management, the household-budget, education, and the proper attitude to teen-age children. At a time when the public seemed to be tired of meetings, these meetings were an enormous success, and they even created contacts with people who would otherwise never have dreamt of accepting an invitation from the Church.

The Young Homes Movement now has centres in most towns and in quite a few country parishes. It has even spread to other countries.

L.Y.M. "More women will go to Heaven than men", the Rev. *Vilh. Beck* once said. Well, it is not up to that zealous protagonist of the Church to settle that. However, if we look at the Danish Church, there is no denying that women do most of the work, fill most of the pews, and are the most frequent guests at the Lord's Supper. This state of affairs drove some men to start *The Laymen's Foreign Mission* whose first endeavour was to put men in touch with the foreign mission, but which has later taken up the work of confronting irreligious men with the Christian faith through special meetings and gatherings. To-day *L.Y.M.* is a wide-awake, energetic wing of the Danish Church. It is able to assemble great numbers of men – especially for the large conferences which are held annually at *Nyborg Strand,* a Danish conference centre which is well-known in other countries, too. These conferences usually attract about a thousand men from the practical walks of life. Here they listen to the Word of God, sing loud enough to send the ceiling flying, have a good and friendly time, and give generous gifts to the Foreign Missions.

The Bible Society and Publishing Houses. It has been said that if St. Paul had lived in the age of the wireless, he would have been able, in one hour, to address more people than he did in all his three mission-journeys. That may be so, but St. Paul's words, and the Bible as a whole, have travelled far as it is, especially by means of the art of printing. The Danish Church has made use of this art, too. We have *The Danish Bible Society* to see that the Holy Scriptures reach as many as possible. Since its foundation in 1814, it has sold 4 million Bibles and separate Bible texts, besides exegeses, and other aids to the study of the Bible. Besides The Danish Bible, the Bible Society also has published Faroese and Greenland translations. In recent years The Bible Society has acknowledged that, in co-operation with *The United Bible Societies,* it has a duty to the millions all over the world who have no Bible in their mother tongue.

While we are speaking of printing, it may be worth mentioning that, considering the smallness of the country, Denmark produces much Christian and Church literature – some of it very valuable. This work is carried on by some publishing-houses which are affiliated with the Home Mission and the Christian Youth Movement.

Radio and Press. The Danish State Radio and Television are important means of evangelization. Every morning, a short service is broadcast, and on Sundays two services. Besides there are often lectures on religious and Church subjects and a running commentary on Church life once a month. Sometimes, too, the State Radio has broadcast a Church Column, to which everybody was invited to send their questions. The questions were of all kinds: Why is there so much suffering in the world? What is the precise meaning of the 6th prayer in "Our Father"? Can Christians go to war? Was Jesus a historic person? What about the Trinity? Why do priests quarrel? Why infant baptism? Is it right for Christians to dance, play cards, etc. Such questions were answered by an experienced and knowledgeable clergyman. The Foreign Missions, too, have figured prominently on Radio and Television programmes. If The State Radio does not itself take the initiative, it is spurred on by *The Christian Radio Listeners' and Television Viewers' Union,* the strongest non-political listeners' organization in Denmark.

And we have the *Kristeligt Dagblad* (Christian Daily), which every day prints not only the usual types of news, but also much information about the Danish and foreign Churches. People from other countries have often been slightly envious when shown The Christian Daily, and it is one of the newspapers most frequently quoted in debates on public affairs. Envy is not an admirable quality, but it is understandable. The *Kristeligt Pressebureau* (Christian News Agency) is worth mentioning, too. It caters for much of the provincial press, *e.g.*, supplying about half of our newspapers with Church News every week.

THE WORK AMONG DANES ABROAD

The Danish Church Abroad. One day a newspaper printed two impressive declarations of love. It was some time after World War II, in South Slesvig, ancient Danish territory but, since the war of 1864, part of Germany. An elderly man said, "We have lost everything (in this case the loss was caused by an incendiary bomb, and he had never received one Pfennig compensation). But I want to tell you this: The only joy we now have, is to go to the service of the Danish church and the social evenings in the Danish school". One Sunday after the service, an old South Slesvigian woman said to the priest, "Once again the best is over. But I am already beginning to look forward to next Sunday – and I never forget to include the priest in my evening-prayers".

Sometimes the question is asked: Is it really necessary for the Church to carry on its work among our countrymen abroad. Isn't it a matter of indifference to Heaven whether a service is held in Danish, German, or English?

However, the gratitude of the two old South Slesvigians makes it clear that there is a real need for the work of the D.K.U. (The Danish Church Abroad). Its aim is stated as follows: "The Danish Church Abroad aims, in co-operation with the Danish National Church, and on an Evangelical Lutheran basis, to work among Danes in foreign parts for the preservation, revival, and strengthening of their faith; as also for the union of all the faithful in well-organized congregations. Besides the work of evangelization, The Danish Church Abroad will endeavour to keep alive, awaken, and strengthen the love of our countrymen for our country, language, and history throughout the ages".

119

The Danish Church Abroad was not founded until 1919, but has for many years carried on its world-wide activities, which are backed by all parts of the Danish National Church. This work is one proof that the Danish Church is not so passive and apathetic as some observers think, but that it is prepared when called upon to serve. Naturally, it is especially active in South Slesvig, where 26 Danish priests and 8 secretaries, and a small number of nursing sisters, are now working for 52 Danish congregations.

This combination of church- and welfare work is also kept up in many of the big cities of Europe, among the many Danish immigrants in Canada, the United States, South America, and lastly – on a modest scale – in Australia and Africa. Several of these places have both a Danish church and a church hall with its youth club, advisory services, etc.

Sailors. "It must really be a strange job to be a sailors' priest, for we sailors are now here, now there, so that his congregation is scattered all over the world". This remark was overheard one day in the stokers' cabin of a ship which a Danish Sailors' priest was visiting. And, in fact, it is.

Two organizations have shared the work, among the sailors: *The Danish Seamen's Church in Foreign Ports* and *The Danish Mission to Seamen.* The former organization has centres, and often churches, too, in many ports. In each a Sailors' priest and his assistant work away, visiting ships, conducting church services, arranging social gatherings ashore, and contacting Danish sailors in hospitals and prisons.

The Danish Mission to Seamen (Indenlandsk Sømandsmission) does not work among sailors in far-away ports, but, nevertheles, among men who are away from their homes. It keeps up nearly fifty Sailors' homes and reading-rooms, scattered in Danish seaports and in the Faroes (and there is, too, one in Grimsby on the English North Sea Coast). The Sailors' Mission also provides various educational facilities for seamen.

A wedding at The Danish Church in Paris.

The Danish Church in the island of Vancouver, British Columbia.

Divine service at the Danish Church of Edmonton, Canada.

From Tanganyika, Bahaya:
Top left: Old church at Karagwe.
Right: Interior of Kaagya Church.
Centre: Christening at Ndolage Hospital Church.
Below: Another, more recently built, church at Karagwe.
Right: The pupils of Ndolage Nursing School.

Arabia:
At top: Holy Communion in The Church of Southern Arabia.

Tanganyika, Buhaya:
Bottom left: Medical examination of schoolboys - to stamp out malaria.
Bottom right: Women attending a course at Kitabe.

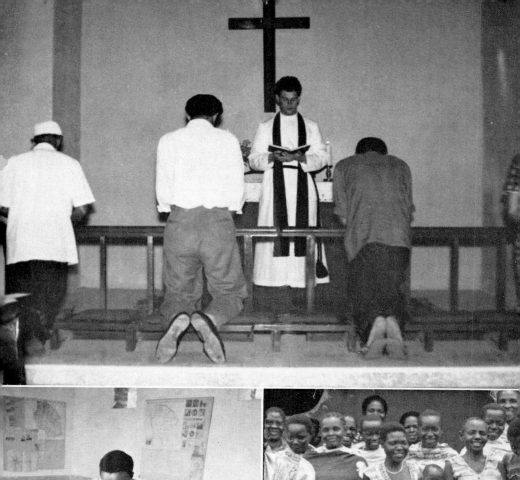

Taiwan: *At top:* Christmas at Lin-chung Road Church. *Below:* Christening at Hsi-chis Church.

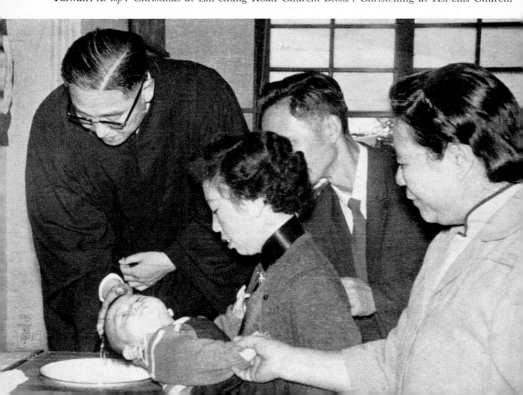

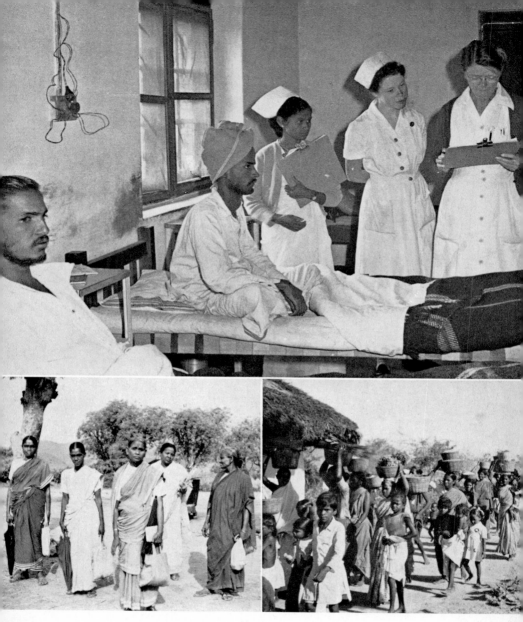

India
At top : Going the rounds at Kotagiri Medical Fellowship.
Bottom left : Bible-women on their way to a village.
Right : Harvest festival at Vaipur.

From FDF's (The Boys' Brigade) Marselisborg camp 1962, attended by
9,000 boys.
Above : Divine service in the camp.
Below : Bird's eye view of the camp, shows Aarhus Bay in the foreground.

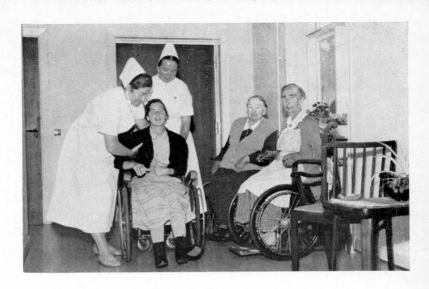

From The Deaconess House of The *Sankt Lukas Stiftelsen* :

Above : Deaconesses at work among chronic invalids.
Below : Child welfare work.

Next page :
From Kofoed's School : four scenes showing the pupils at work to regain their selfrespect. (Page 123).

WELFARE WORK

The Parish Charity Work, the Church Army, etc. "Very rightly our Lutheran Church has attached the greatest importance to the ministry of the Word. For, if the Word be not preached, and the Sacraments not administered, the Church will die. But the duty of the Church is not fulfilled by the preaching and hearing of the Gospel. The Body of Christ has many members, all called upon to help each other. Where the Word is active, the deed will follow. Loving helpfulness should be the emblem of the Church. So one of the primary duties of the Church to-day is to put the Diaconate in its proper place, the place to which its importance for the life of Church entitles it. Only when the Word and active charity are combined, will the Gospel of the Life-to-Come be proclaimed with full force".

The ideal which inspired these words of a bishop, the Church has tried in a number of ways to live up to. But is there any need of the Church's charity work, the practical demonstration of love of one's neighbour in Denmark to-day? Not so long ago, *Negley Farson* said: "That country is probably the most highly developed welfare state in the world". Others have made equally flattering remarks, and there is no denying that the social services in Denmark are highly developed. The sick, unemployed, or aged are looked after by the public authorities. It is, nevertheless, common experience that, where the welfare services are the sole means of relief, life is apt to become slightly cold and grey for those who, for some reason, have recourse to them. For those who need help also need that warmth of human fellowship which is a reflection of God's love of man. Further, there will always be some who are in need of help, without being qualified for public assistance. This is where the Church comes in.

Its welfare work is partly carried out by *the Association of Parochial Social Services* (De samvirkende Menighedsplejer) which in many parishes try to come to the assistance of the aged, the cronic invalids, and the poor. This Association of Parish Social Services has always been very enterprising. It has started nursing homes, brought food to the homes of the sick, provided summer-holidays in the country for the aged, and engaged occupational therapists to keep the sick actively occupied by hobbies or light work. Mention should also be made of *Alfred Th. Jørgensen,* the first secretary of the Federation. He was a pioneer of the Church charities in this country, who worked for the establishment of the first children's welfare centres (*vide* above page 108). The next secretary *W. Westergaard Madsen,* besides being active in other fields, was instrumental to the setting up of pedicure centres here and there in the capital, so that old people could get treatment for their feet. Such a centre has even been opened in some rooms of the episcopal mansion, residence of the one-time secretary, who is now Bishop of Copenhagen.

The Church Army (Kirkens Korshær), modelled on the English Church Army, has primarily tried to succour alcoholics, ex-convicts, anti-social persons, or other unfortunates. It employs no less than sixty or seventy permanent staff, of which four are priests, besides hundreds of volunteers who give up their spare-time to unpaid work for the Church Army. Often this work has been particularly blessed. And nowhere in this country, so it is said, does the hymn-singing ring out more enthusiastically, than from the homeless, the drunks, and tramps who are gathered for their church service. It is a common experience of the Danish Church that the higher the social level of a congregation, the poorer is the hymn-singing!

A few years ago, the *Church Army* entered upon a new task: *The St. Nicolai Service,* so called after the Church of St. Nicolai, which is the headquarters of the Army. The aim of this service is not to do missionary work in the ordinary sense of the word, but at all hours of the day and night to be prepared to listen and talk to persons needing this help. "Call me, if you are thinking of suicide", the leader of the Church Army once said in a newspaper-interview. Such an invitation indicates that the Church Army's aim is to provide at least one place where there is always a little human kindness to be found, where no one need be afraid of being regarded as a nuisance, or of applying outside office hours. Those who apply for help in person or by telephone, can rely on their anonymousness being respected, no introduction being necessary. Further, all who work for the Nicolai Service, about 120 priests and an equal number of lay-men have placed themselves at its disposal, are bound over by prom-ises of secrecy.

There might be reason to mention several other kinds of Christian services, such as *Blue Cross, the Christian Temperance League, the Skovtofte Homes,* for young girls who have got the wrong start in life, various institutions which aid homeless men, and *The Christian Students' Settlement,* situated in one of the most densely populated Copenhagen districts. Here a group of young university men and women gather young and old in clubs and meetings, occupying their minds with lectures, classes, and discussions.

KOFOED'S SCHOOL AND FALK HANSENS SOCIAL WORK

"Knocked Out – No!" is the title of an autobiography by *Hans Christian Kofoed,* the parish clerk, who never could pass by a fellow-human who was in need of a helping hand. With his two empty hands – and a fervent trust in God – he took up the welfare work among the Capital's unemployed and often unemployable men (most of them immigrants from the provinces and, consequently, home-less). From very modest beginnings he created his *School for the workless,* which is one of the most spectacular Danish attempts to help the workless and give them a fresh start. Of course, Kofoed had to contend with great difficulties and much scepticism. However, he kept up the struggle, and built the school which, on Christian principles, helps the unemployed to help themselves. The idea of the school is that – in order to receive aid in the form of food and clothes from the school – a man must first himself have undergone a cleaning (bath, hair-cut, shave, etc.) and given his clothes a similar treatment in the school's laundry, tailors' room, or shoemakers' workshop. Gradually, round this core, many other departments have grown up: workshops, a "vitamin inn", welfare office, and a *training school for the workless* where a considerable number of young unemployed men can get board, lodgings, instruction, and work. Besides, Kofoed's School arranges several courses, folk-highschool evenings, etc.

Mention should also be made of another special kind of Christian welfare work. In the inter-war years, the Copenhagen Y.M.C.A. asked a young theologian *Aage Falk Hansen* to arrange some evening entertainments for the workless, of whom there were in those years shockingly great numbers. He accepted on condition that it was for that winter of 1928 only. However, once he had started, the work gripped him, and he could never give it up.

How was he to tackle the job? In the Y.M.C.A. festival hall there sat about a thousand men, old and young. Even the young looked old and many faces wore expressions of dull despair. Against this compact mass of inertia, Falk Hansen had to contend, and he tried all the means at his disposal to stimulate the self-respect and raise the spirits of the unemployed. At last, smiles spread over the faces of the audience. This was the beginning of a hectic activity which lasted all through the winter months of that and successive years. The meetings were held in concert halls, cinemas, and mission houses, and gradually the work expanded. A club was started for such as were prepared to share the responsibilities, an advisory office was set up, and a summer camp. All this set the example for much successful work of the same kind both in Copenhagen and the provinces.

One evening, Falk Hansen, with the assistance of the members of the club, invited the unemployed and all Copenhagen workers to a service in the cathedral — and the cathedral was packed with workers, which had never happened before.

What have been the fruits of these labours? Not only that the morale of many fellow-countrymen was improved, so that they tackled the difficulties of their existence with renewed vigour. Not only had a very important breach been made in the wall of passive spiritual indifference or obdurate hostility which had enclosed large sections of the working classes. But now there was also, in many circles, a willingness to hear the word of Jesus Christ.

Deaconesses and Deacons. In the Anglican Church deaconesses are a kind of assistant priests, whose duty it is to read the morning-

and evening prayers in church, to teach and preach (but not to celebrate Holy Communion). The deaconesses of the Danish Church, on the other hand, by the work of their hands, help those who need such services. This was the function of the deaconesses of the first Christian communities, and of those who took up the work when the order of deaconesses was revived in Germany about the middle of the 19th century. It has been rightly maintained that the order of deaconesses and deacons is an ecclesiastical office beside the priesthood. This assertion is justifiable because the diaconate has a character and sphere of activity of its own, which is quite different from the preacher's.

So the deaconesses are the handmaidens of the Church, who are to transform the Grace of God into practical service of their neighbour.

There are in Denmark three *Deaconess Houses: Den Danske Diakonissestiftelse, Sankt Lukas Stiftelsen,* and one which is affiliated with the *Philadelphia Colony,* a large hospital for mental patients and epileptics. The total number of sisters is about 700, who are employed by hospitals, orphanages, etc. directly affiliated with the deaconess houses. Besides, in many parts of the country, they carry on the work of nursing the sick and aged, children and physically disabled. A few deaconesses work for the Foreign Missions, and a little band works among our fellow-countrymen in South Slesvig.

Now, what is a Deaconess House? First of all, it is the sisters who have entered it to serve, and who after some years' probation are consecrated in the church for this particular kind of the Church's day-to-day work. The sisters are easily recognizable by their fine – and clerical – dress. They live in a state of economic equality and remain unmarried in order to devote all their time and energies to the service. Further it can be said that a Deaconess House is a *training centre.* It is open, too, to young girls – who are not planning to become deaconesses. It is a *home* which, in all respects – spiritually, economically, etc. supports the sisters, no matter where they are working. It is a *community* of a special kind. So a Deaconess House is not "a convent or a refuge for those who want to escape from worldly cares. It is an armoury which equips the sisters for their service in the world; a place where they are taught preparedness to go forth whenever there is a call for their services. Lastly, it is, too, the home and community needful for their services".

Likewise, nearly seven hundred *deacons* wish, through their activities, to help propagate the Gospel. Denmark has two schools for deacons, one in Aarhus and one affiliated with the Philadelphia Colony. They are open to young men who wish to take up work among the sick and disabled, among the destitute and among alcoholics, and others who are in need of help. After three years' training, the young deacons are ordained.

Unlike the deaconesses, the deacons themselves apply for their positions and receive their salaries, just as they are free to marry. The large majority of them take up work among the sick and disabled. Quite a few become secretaries of various youth organizations, managers of soldiers' homes, sacristans, or enter the Service of the Foreign Missions. The deacons who have graduated from our two Deacons' Schools are members of two Brotherhoods, which at regular intervals have conventions together and publish a magazine for their members.

Church of Denmark Inter-Church Aid Committee (Den Danske Folkekirkes Nødhjælp). *Karen Jeppe,* known in large parts of the world as *the Danish Girl* for her work in the first decades of this century among Armenian refugees, once, in Geneva, when the almost insurmountable difficulties of the task were being discussed, changed the mood of all those present by the words: "It is but a little candle, but the night is so dark."

It is still very dark in many places. Besides, by means of television, and the Press, sufferings and distress throughout the world are brought home to us. Seen against the background of the world's poverty and sufferings, it is but a little candle the Danish Church has been able to light. At least it has realized that sufferers throughout this wide world are our brothers, and that we have a duty to them. *Church of Denmark Inter-Church Aid Committee* only set to work about forty years ago. At first its main preoccupation was the needs of Lutheran minorities who often lived in very poor and difficult circumstances. But later on the Danish Church has eagerly joined in the efforts to relieve destitution in Asia, the Near East, and Africa. First of all, in close co-operation with The Lutheran World Federation, of which the Danish Church is a member, we have been engaged in relief work among the Arab refugees in Jordan and Syria. Danish deaconesses, too, have worked there, and other Danish contributions have consisted in considerable supplies of milk powder, clothes, and hospital equipment – just in order to light a little candle in "the night which is so dark".

THE FOREIGN MISSIONS AND THE ECUMENICAL MOVEMENT

Danish Mission Societies. A Danish missionary once gave the following description of a meeting in Numan: "Matthias, the first speaker, climbs on to the platform. With some others, he had been visiting five towns. He mentions their names, and we, who are sitting on the benches, know them. Small towns, all of them, hidden away in the African wilderness, but each a world unto itself, where men and women are born and die, where some are born to rule and others to obey, where striving and suffering are the common lot – until the inhabitants close their eyes without a hope. In each town they had been received with the cry, "When will a helper (evangelist) come to us?" They had answered: "Each of us has his village, but we shall ask the young men of the congregation." – Now Matthias asked the question. It penetrated to the very hearts of the audience. He concluded his simple story with an account of what the inhabitants of the last town had said to him: When your Lord comes and finds us in our sinful state, we will say, "Nobody came to put our feet upon the right path; that is why we do not know it!" What is your answer to this? Matthias concluded. Have you come merely to be told about it, or will you do something about it?"

There are many within the Danish Church who, in childhood or youth, in the Sunday school or youth club, have listened to such stories and understood that Matthias' words were not only addressed to his countrymen. They are addressed to any one who has heard the words of Our Lord: "Full authority in heaven and on earth has been committed to me. Go forth, therefore, and make all nations my disciples". Let us hope that there are many of our countrymen who know the full implications of this command to go forth also to those who do not know of such questions as those asked in Numan.

Even if Denmark must be given credit for being the first Lutheran country to start the Foreign Mission – in 1705 the Danish King at his Government's expense sent two missionaries to Tranquebar in India – the voluntary mission did not get really started, until after the foundation of *The Danish Mission Society* in 1821.

There are now in Denmark 14 mission societies, large and small, plus some aid committees. These 14 support about 250 missionaries and their work. To this must be added the rather extensive work carried out for the Danish Free Churches by about fifty missionaries.

Not only the oldest, but by far the largest is *The Danish Mission Society*. It has sent missionaries to the Arcot District and East Jeypore in India, South Arabia, Tanganyika in Africa, Taiwan on Formosa, and to Japan. Until the Communists took over, The D.M.S. had for many years carried on successful work in China. Other important mission societies are *The United Danish Mission to the Sudan,* and *The Moravian Brethren's Danish Mission Society,* both of which work in Africa, *Danish Mission to the Orient* (Østerlandsmissionen), which works among the Moslems of Syria, and *The Danish Mission among the Santals,* which has a district of its own in the delta of the Ganges in North East India. *The Mission to the Buddhists* at first worked among the Buddhists of China, and now in Japan. *The Mission to the Jews* like The Mission to the Orient, has learned the truth of these works of *Lewis Way:* "To be able to accomplish something, one has to have more faith than Abraham, more endurance than Moses, and more patience than Job".

Several Danish Mission Societies do not limit their activities to the propagation of the Gospel. They have also set up schools for children and adolescents, opened clinics, founded hospitals, *e.g.* for lepers, and sanatoria for consumptives.

Each mission society is backed by wide circles in the home country, who support its work through prayers, keen interest, and splendid generosity. At present, it is the subject of lively discussion whether it would not be better to amalgamate all these societies, which so far have each had their separate governing boards, work on the home front, finances, and printing expenses. Perhaps the chief reason for this discussion is the realization that the Foreign Missions concern the whole Church, nay, that the view that *The Church is Mission,* can be more efficiently propagated, if the work of doing so becomes less a matter of "private enterprise".

Since 1912, we have had a *Danish Missions Council,* on which the various mission societies are represented. This Council arranges joint meetings for the Foreign Missions, and courses for missionaries visiting the home country. It tries to avoid rivalry between the mission societies, and to work for co-operation. During the two World Wars, the Council proved of signal importance as an organization that could speak up for the missionaries' interests both to the Danish Government, the Governments of Foreign Powers, and to other mission societies.

The Ecumenical Movement. In recent years, on a January evening, the streets of central Copenhagen have been more than usually crowded. Large crowds swarmed first to *St. Paul's Church* (which belongs to the National Church), and next they paid a visit to the Methodists' *Jerusalem Church.* Afterwards the tour included the Orthodox *Alexander Newsky Church,* the Roman Catholic *St. Ansgar's Church,* the Anglican *St. Alban's Church* and finally the Swedish *Gustav's Church.*

In each church these peripatetic church-goers joined in short prayers – and in the last one listened to no less than three speakers: A Roman Catholic, a Lutheran, and a Reformed priest.

They looked very much alike these pilgrims, as they walked shivering through the cold streets. But inside their clothes they, like the angels of Heaven, were of many kinds. They belonged to various churches, which had formerly striven in vain to bear with each other. Yet now that they had all joined the ecumenical church tour, they did experience some of the happiness of Christian Unity.

The Ecumenical Movement has survived difficult times in Denmark as elsewhere. There were days when Danes were convinced that Lutheran Christianity was the only road to salvation. At the close of the 19th century, however, the idea of Christian Unity began to gain ground. One reason for this was the international *Evangelical Alliance,* of which many Danes are still members. For, if agreement could not be reached about anything else, it should, at least, be possible to *pray together!*

It was, however, not until after the Great Church Convention in Stockholm, in 1925, that the Ecumenical Movement really began to get going. Especially after World War II, it became increasingly clear to many that "the Ecumenical Movement is not an ecclesiastical hobby, which one can cultivate or leave alone to suit one's taste. On the contrary, the Unity of the Church is the will of God. The old hostility between the Churches, the mutual accusations of heresy, are sins, which we cannot atone for, but in which we cannot persist". When a Church has become aware of this fact, the Ecumenical Movement becomes an indispensable part of its daily life.

There are in Denmark increasing numbers of people engaged in the ecumenical work. Many young persons join study circles and the summer camps arranged for the young of various Churches. Many, both theologians and laymen take part in the meeting and conferences which are being held all over the world – from which, as a rule, they return not only with rich intellectual profits and souls filled with inspiration, but also astounded that it has not yet become a natural thing for all participants in such a meeting to partake of the Lord's Supper together.

We have in Denmark *Church of Denmark Council on Inter-Church Relations,* which handles the Danish National Church's relations with other Churches all over the world: *The Ecumenical Council of Churches in Denmark* (Det økumeniske Fællesraad) which is responsible for the relations between the country's National Church and the Free Churches and their united representations in their relations with other Churches. There is *Denmark's Ecumenical Youth Council* whose task it is to inspire the young with the understanding of, and preparedness to work for Church unity. Finally, there is, too, the already mentioned *Danish Mission Council,* which is now an integral part of the Ecumenical Movement.

EPILOGUE

A young American negress had for a year been the guest pupil of a Danish high school. Before her departure, she was interviewed by one of her school-fellows. In reply to a question about her view of Danish religion, she said, "I can only produce some theories as to why Danes are less religious than Americans. One would think that the average Dane has got too used to having a Church, when it suits him, without being responsible for it".

Evidently, she, too, had discovered the lack of proportion with the mention of which we started this chapter. The disproportion between the 95 per cent membership, and the apparently small number of those who share the life the Church. And, for that matter, she is quite right. A Dane can use the Church when it suits him, without having to assume responsibility for it. The church is right there, and the services go on, whether people enter or not. And the priest is there, whether the people seem to need him or not. No, there is no need to assume responsibility for the Church. The whole machinery is there, no matter what we do. It is paid for by the Church tax, etc.

It is to be hoped, however, that this account of the Danish Church's manifold activities, will show the reader that the contact between the Church and the average Dane is more extensive and more intimate than the casual visitor, who may only become acquainted with one *milieu,* will be in a position to realize. Indeed, that there are many who not only are "used to having a Church which they can use as it suits them", but who are also prepared to shoulder their share of responsibility for the life of the Church.

There are two final questions to be dealt with. The first is: Who pays for all this gratis preaching, teaching, and welfare work?

Recently, during one of the annual conventions of one of the Church organizations great financial difficulties had to be faced. Urgent problems had to be solved, but where to find the money?

It had been hoped that the Government would open its coffers, but of late the State had been rather chary of contributions. Then the last decade's excellent Minister for the Danish National Church, Mrs. *Bodil Koch,* took the floor and said, "Do it yourselves! Surely, the members of the Church would be able to raise a couple of millions, if they really wanted to. And it would be a salutary lesson to the sluggish Government machinery, if the problem was solved in that way".

In this context be it said that, to a very large extent, the Church people have "done it themselves" – and are still doing it. True, the authorities do not stint in expenses *e.g.* for the work of the Church among Danes in South Slesvig – or among sailors in foreign ports. It is also true that the Church's educational and welfare activities, like other work in these fields is supported by Government grants. However, in the free work of evangelization and mission among children and adolescents, as also among non-Christians in the mission fields – or in the efforts to find new ways to relieve material or spiritual distress – that is, the pioneer work – in all this the Church people, who more or less actively share the life of the Church, in large organizations or small circles have got to "do it themselves". And again they have done it. Thus *e.g.* voluntary contributions to the Danish Foreign Missions every year amount to about kr. 7.000.000.

The second question: what are the relations between the official National Church and all the voluntary Church activities? About these relations there are almost exclusively good things to be said. Even if, *e.g.,* there is no organizational link between the official National Church and the many societies, associations, and institutions, both the Church Ministry and the top leaders of the Church always show great sympathy and readiness to help. We shall only mention a couple of facts: We regard it as a matter of course that the Mission

Societies, which are entirely independent of the Church, can ordain and send out their missionaries from a church. And afterwards we regard these missionaries as the ambassadors of the Danish Church. And we regard it as a matter of course that the revival movement of The Home Mission, which often acts as the Church's bad conscience, nay, its stern accuser, opens its annual conventions in a church. It is even taken for granted that a cathedral dean welcomes the visitors and addresses to them a few good words to remember while they are at work. We also take it as a matter of course that on Easter Sunday in most Danish churches a collection is taken for the Christian Youth Movement, which, formally, is not in any way subject to the authority of the Church Minister. Lastly, without being members *ex officio* – many bishops and priests are on the committees of all these voluntary activities.

Once upon a time – it was about the turn of the century – all these voluntary and "private" Church activities were making great strides. This seemed to be where things were happening. – Now times have changed. The circumstances which gave rise to all this, no longer exist. Now things have returned to normal again, bringing quiet growth in some places, stagnation and regression in others.

However, in good times or bad, for all the activities which we have here recorded, the Danish Church is not so stagnant or out of touch with people as foreigners often have thought and said. And surely it will not become so, as long as we have this interplay between the National Church as an institution and all the Church activities which are carried out on a voluntary basis.

OTHER CHURCHES IN DENMARK

The Roman Catholic Church

After the victory of the Evangelical Lutheran Reformation of 1536 the Roman Catholic Church was prohibited in Denmark until the adoption of the Free Constitution of 1849, which granted freedom of religion to Danish citizens. In the period between 1536 and 1849 Catholic worship was only permitted under the auspices of the diplomatic representatives of Catholic countries.

When, in 1849, religious liberty had been introduced, foreign priests and nuns were allowed to enter the country. They were the founders of the Roman Catholic Church which we find in Denmark to-day. About the turn of the century with the conversions of Johannes Jørgensen, the poet, and Mogens Ballin, the painter, the Catholic congregation becomes more emphatically Danish. While, in the "pioneer period" there had been a large foreign element in the congregations, this century has seen an increase in the number of Danish members. To-day the large majority of Catholic Christians in this country are Danes.

The membership of the Catholic Church in Denmark is estimated at 26.000. Since 1939 the Church has been led by a Danish Benedictine, Theodor Suhr, as Bishop. In 1953 Denmark became an independent diocese with Copenhagen as its Cathedral city. While preparations were being made for the Second Vatican Council, Bishop Theodor Suhr was a member of the Cathedral Committee as representative of the Roman Catholic Church of Scandinavia.

Some of the work of the Catholic Church in Denmark is carried out in schools and hospitals. As part of the Danish educational and hospital services both activities receive Government grants. Several schools have lay headmasters and sisters and priests on their staffs, working on equal terms with laymen. There are in Denmark about 120 Catholic priests, of whom 30 are Danes. The rest come from

France, Germany, Holland, Belgium, the United States, England, Austria, and Switzerland.

The organizations, which are mostly run by laymen, are another important field. The Catholic Youth organizations are permanent observers in Denmark's Ecumenical Youth Council, whose president is either a member of the National Church or of one of the Free Churches.

In Copenhagen's Bredgade we find St. Ansgar's Bookshop, which is the Catholic bookshop of Denmark, and Niels Stensen's Library. Both places give detailed information of Catholic Faith and life. Besides, hotels catering for foreign visitors are given hours and addresses for Catholic church services. In some of the Catholic churches of Copenhagen and its suburbs mass is celebrated throughout the summer in French and English. In Copenhagen and some of the larger provincial towns there are Vespers on Sunday afternoons or evenings.

The office of the Catholic Bishop of Denmark is at 7, Frederiksgade, Copenhagen K.

By *Walter Dalland,* Birkerød.

The Methodist Church in Denmark

Among the countless immigrants who, throughout the 19th century, poured into the new World, when the "America fever" swept the countries of Europe, there were also tens of thousands of Scandinavians, trying to launch upon new careers in America. Among these immigrants we find Chr. Willerup, a young Danish business man, born in Copenhagen in 1815. He prospered over there. At the early age of thirty-two he took over a substantial business in Strassburg, Ohio. There he came into contact with Methodism, and shortly after his conversion he accepted a call from the Church to join in the work among the numerous Danish, Swedish, and Norwegian immigrants.

A few years later the leaders of the Church asked if he was willing to go to Norway as leader of the mission which had recently been started there. On July 2nd 1856 he landed in Norway.

For years the thought of going to Copenhagen and making an attempt to start the work there had been preparing in Willerup's mind. So one day in July 1858 he arrived in the city of his childhood.

On Sunday, August 8th 1858, he held his first church service in a diminutive hall behind 21 Store Kongensgade, which, among other organizations, had housed the "Dansk Samfund". Willerup was an eloquent preacher, and before long this hall was too small. So, of course, he soon began making plans for a church-building, and found a site for it on the corner of Rigensgade and Stokhusgade.

Only six months after Willerup's first church service, he could organize the first Methodist congregation in Denmark. That was on January 11th 1859. The membership was very small, at first. However, there was a little flock of friends and adherents, so, gradually, the congregation increased considerably. Then, on August 7th 1866, the Jerusalem church in Copenhagen was consecrated on the said site.

Even before the church had been built Willerup applied for Government recognition of the Methodist church in Denmark. A long time was to elapse, before this goal was attained. But on September 22nd 1865 the Methodist Church was recognized by Royal Decree, *i. e.* religious ceremonies performed by this Church are legally valid, it has the right to keep authorized church registers and issue certificates of baptisms, weddings, etc.

In the provinces the work spread with the same rapidity as in Copenhagen. Vejle in Jutland founded the second Danish Methodist Congregation in Denmark on May 12th 1861. The third was organized at Svendborg in the island of Funen on May 10, 1862. So the work was continued, and to-day the Church numbers about 3500 adult members. It has 36 churches or church halls, in the following localities: Copenhagen 3, The Jerusalem Church in the Østerbro District, Betania Church in Møllegade, Nørrebro District; and the Golgatha Church, Kong Georg's Allé, Frederiksberg. In the island of Zealand 5: at Elsinore, Karlslunde, Holbæk, Slagelse, and Kalundborg. The island of Bornholm has 5: at Allinge, Åkirkeby, Pedersker, Rønne and Nexø. In Funen 5: at Svendborg, Fåborg, Rudkøbing and 2 at Odense. Jutland has 17 at Vejle, Give, Vonge, Silkeborg,

Horsens, Århus, Randers, Aalborg, Brønderslev, Hjørring, Løkken, Frederikshavn, Strandby, Lemvig, Holstebro, Varde, and Esbjerg. A total of 87 places where the Gospel is preached, served by 21 ministers and about 70 lay preachers.

The Work Among Children and Adolescents. The first small beginnings of the Sunday School work within the Methodist Church took place in 1860 in Copenhagen. It was, however, only after the new church had been built that the work really got going. At all the places where the work prospered, Sunday Schools were set up. So there are now 35 Sunday Schools.

The first youth organization was started in Vejle in 1892. Before long all congregations of any size at all had their own youth organizations, to-day there are 24 youth organizations, with a membership of about 1300.

About the turn of the century the *Ungdomsforbundet* took up other work among the not too young children, the junior organizations. In 1922 both the Boy Scout and Girl Guide Movements were started. They now have independent National Divisions within the Y.M.C.A. and Y.W.C.A. Scouts. There are at present 1200 scouts and juniors.

Publishing House. The Church runs a small publishing house. Among its publications are *Methodistkirkens Ugeblad* (The Methodist Weekly), the *Vårbrud* (organ of the youth-organizations), the *Methodist-Kvinden* (a missions periodical), the *Kammeraten* (the Sunday School), *Centralmissionens Blad,* and The Danish edition of "The Upper Room", a devotional tract.

Welfare Work. When the Methodist Church had taken shape in Denmark – the Methodist tradition, heritage, and faith – it began to take up welfare and philanthropic work on a small scale. In 1879 the Rev. C. F. Eltzholz of Vejle started the first Temperance League, the mother organization of the entire Temperance Movement in Denmark. In 1906 the first infant home, *Marielund,* near Vejle, was opened. This was the beginning of extensive child welfare work, which to-day includes a Home for Mothers and Children – *"Dear Home"* –

at Hellerup; the infant homes of *Brinken,* at Vejle; *Willeruplund,* at Odense; *Fjordbakken,* at Holbæk; *Marielund,* at Vejle; a home for older children, *Fremtidshåb,* at Frederikshavn; a home for backward children, *Ålykkegård,* at Odense; *Gersonshøj,* a home for mentally defective children, at Hellerup; and the Central Mission's day-nursery and kindergarten beside the Jerusalem Church.

1907 saw the beginning of the nursing sisters' activities. In the course of time, the nursing sisters have been very active in nursing-societies, health insurance societies, child welfare organizations, and, last but not least, in nursing homes and nursing sisters' homes, of which there are two in Århus and two in Copenhagen.

In 1910 the Rev. A. Bast started the Central Mission. It began when the rooms in the church basement were opened to homeless men, of whom, especially in those days, there were great numbers in Copenhagen. To-day the Central Mission costs millions. It comprises the usual welfare- and relief-work, free dinners, reading and hobby-rooms for the unemployed, homes for mothers and infants, a crèche, kindergarten, a home for mentally defective children, a youth centre, and a home for the aged. Further, the *Solborgen,* a holiday camp situated near Sejrø Bay.

In several of the larger provincial towns, too, such philanthropic work is carried on as distribution of clothes, food, etc.

Like all other Methodist churches, the Methodist Church of Denmark is a Free Church, independent of the Government. Its doctrine is based upon the Apostolic Creed and its fundamental dogma John Wesley's Twenty-FourArticles, extracted and revised from theThirty-Nine Articles of the Anglican Church. Its system of government, too, is like that of the other Methodist Churches. With Norway, Sweden, and Finland it makes up the North European Episcopal Area (Central Conference). Its Bishop is Bishop Odd Hagen, Stockholm.

Numerically the Methodist Church of Denmark is but small. Nevertheless, in the years which have elapsed since its foundation, it has made its contribution to Danish church life, and its influence has been considerable, especially on philanthropy and welfare work.

By the Rev. *Eigil Carlsen,* Hjørring.

The Baptist Union of Denmark

Denmark is traditionally a Lutheran country. Until 1849 the inhabitants of Denmark were not allowed to adopt any other religion. The Danish Church had for centuries been a State Church, and very few even dreamt of changing this situation. So it came as a shock to the Church Authorities when, in October 1839, a Baptist Church was founded. It immediately met with oppression, members being fined, imprisoned, etc. However, the Baptist Church struggled on, and even spread to various parts of the country. In 1849, the Danish Parliament passed the Basic Law in which was laid down the country's new Constitution, thus introducing religious liberty, although the Lutheran Church still remained the privileged Church. Then the Baptits numbered about 500. At the present time, the Baptist Union of Denmark numbers about 7300 adult members of 42 congregations with 37 ministers and 80 lay preachers. In Burundi-Rwanda two Unions of Baptist Churches have been established by Danish Baptist missionaries. At present there are 18 Danish missionaries working in the same area.

It is a remarkable historical fact that the Baptist Union of Denmark was not founded by foreign missionaries. The small group that, in 1839, established the first Baptist church in this country had adopted Baptist convictions through their own independent, unguided Bible-studies. Individuals who, for various reasons, had been dissatisfied with the State Church and its beliefs, had got in touch with each other and met in a Copenhagen home for Bible study and prayer. Some of them were still church-goers, others came from groups who met regularly for Bible study under the guidance of laymen who, though critical, were still loyal to the Church. This group could not, however, adjust themselves to the existing Church, but did not know how to break away from it, or what to put in its place. They were not aware of the existence in England and Germany of Baptist Churches whose views were similar to their own. A Dane named Julius Købner had become acquainted with the Baptist Church of Hamburg in Germany in 1836. Afterwards he got to know the above-mentioned group in 1839 when travelling about

Denmark as a missionary. He found their meeting-place and was able to inform them that they shared the beliefs of the Baptists. Later that year, on the early morning of October 27th, Y. G. Oncken, minister of the Hamburg church, baptized 11 persons in a lake in Copenhagen. They celebrated the Lord's Supper, and a Baptist Church was founded. In their view the Lutheran doctrine of Church and Sacraments was out of harmony with New Testament teaching that Baptism and Church were a Fellowship of Believers. A man had to be *called* by the Holy Spirit to a Baptism which meant becoming a disciple of Christ, not *brought* to an entirely impersonal act. The Church as the Body of Christ was to be governed by confessing Christians. Every member was a "priest", with responsibility for the life and teachings of the Church. To these early Baptists the Church was a spiritual democracy based on the authority of Scripture.

From these early beginnings as a small lay-movement the Baptists have developed into the largest Evangelical Free Church in Denmark. The *Christ Church* of Baggesensgade, Copenhagen, can trace its history back to the small Church of 1839. The *Købner-Kirken* in Shetlandsgade, Copenhagen S., and the *Fredskirken* in Howitsvej, Copenhagen F., are other Baptist churches in the central part of the city. They are both offsprings of the old Church, founded in the nineties. The Copenhagen suburbs of Hvidovre, Herlev, and Lyngby have their own Baptist churches.

Besides the regular Sunday services, which are open to every one in each of these churches, there are all sorts of activities in the course of the week; e. g. Sunday schools, scout meetings, clubs for children. Outside Copenhagen there are Baptist churches in most of the larger towns and in some of the farming districts. *Tølløse Højskole* (Tølløse Highschool) is an educational centre for students of theology, church-workers, or young people who want a secondary education or a folk-highschool course. Shortly, a "Baptists' House" in Cophenhagen (Worsaaesvej), will be built to house the theological seminary, press, etc. The office of the Union's General Secretary is in Copenhagen.

The Baptist Union of Denmark is a member of the Ecumenical

Council of Denmark, The World Council of Churches, and the Evangelical Alliance. *The Baptist Press* (Baptisternes Forlag) publishes periodicals and books on the life and faith of the Baptists.

By the Rev. *K. Kyrø-Rasmussen,* Copenhagen.

FREE CHURCHES IN DENMARK

Adventistsamfundet (The Seventh Day Adventists)
Address: 10, Svanevej, København NV.

Den Apostolske Kirke i Danmark (The Apostolic Church)
Address: 31, Blegdamsvej, København Ø.
Congregation affiliated with English Pentecostal Movement.

Frelsens Hær (Salvation Army)
Address: 9, Frederiksbergallé, Copenhagen V.

Det Danske Missionsforbund (The Mission Covenant Church of Denmark)
Address: 17, Kapelvej, Copenhagen N.
A Congregational Free Church stemming from the 19th century revival movement in Denmark and affiliated with corresponding Mission Societies in the other Scandinavian countries. Missions in Thailand.

Pinsebevægelsen (The Pentecostal Movement)
Address: Elimforsamlingen: 7, Kronprinsensgade, Copenhagen K.
Tabor Menigheden: 62, Lyngbyvej, Copenhagen Ø.

SELECTED LIST OF
DANISH CHURCH ORGANIZATIONS

This chapter gives a summary of a number of Church organizations working in close co-operation with the National Church. It has not been possible to list all organizations, but this extract should give the reader some idea of extensive activities in Church's Missions, nursing services, etc.

Det Danske Bibelselskab (Danish Bible Society)
Address: 67, Købmagergade, Copenhagen K.
Founded 1814.
Aim: The dissemination of the Bible and individual parts of the Bible in translations authorized by the Church and at low prices, or – in certain circumstances – gratis. Besides the Society backs organizations for Bible-reading and Bible-study.
President: Prefect Ove Larsen. Total staff: 15.
Budget: circa kr. 200.000. Annual turnover about kr. 800.000. Funds collected: kr. 150–200.000.

Dansk Bibelskole (The Danish Bible School)
Address: 10, Frederiksberg allé, Copenhagen V.
Founded 1912.
Aim: To support the members of the congregation in their efforts to acquire a wide knowledge, understanding of, and insight into the Word of God and to enable them to study the Bible individually.
Chairman: Professor N. H. Søe, D.D. President: the Rev. Ib Lindegreen Andersen of Messiaskirken. Staff: The teaching staff is made up of a large number of priests, teachers, professors, missionaries, and others.
Budget: The Bible-School is self-supporting, costs being paid with the interest of its own capital. It provides morning-, afternoon-, and

evening courses, and also correspondence courses. In Copenhagen and suburbs there are parish-courses, and in the provinces provincial courses. Affiliated with the Bible-School is the Collection of Materials which runs a permanent exhibition of books and other teaching aids for religious instruction, youth work, and Sunday-school work. Besides, it sells educational material.

Det Blå Kors (The Blue Cross) (Denmark's Christian Temperance League)
Address: 109, Gothersgade, Copenhagen K.
Founded 1895.
Purpose: The protection of the young, rescuing alcoholists, combatting existing drinking-habits.
Chairman: The Rev. Børge E. Andersen, Secretary: Secretary-General P. Hansen. Total staff: 25–30.
Budget: kr. 1.033.093. Means collected: kr. 197.670. The B. K. includes 362 local branches all over Denmark. It is the Church Temperance League and part of the international league of the same name. In Denmark it runs two clinics and two nursing homes for alcoholists.

*Indenlandsk Sømandsmission (*Danish Mission to Seamen)
Address: 21, Bernstorffsgade, Copenhagen V. Founded in 1905.
Aim: To provide sailors of all nationalities with homes in various ports, where they cand find Christian care and hear the Word of God. Chairman: The Rev. William Larsen, parish priest, Aalborg. Secretary: Secretary-General, seamen's minister, the Rev. Fr. V. Eilschou Holm. Staff: 50 married couples, and two unmarried persons. The total budget is paid for by funds collected, the Sailors' Mission receives no public grant.

De Unge Hjems Bevægelse i Danmark (Young Homes' Movement)
Address: Skaade, Højbjerg. Founded in 1939.
Aim: On the principles of the Danish National Church to guide young families to Christian lives, which is attempted by gathering

about the Christian Gospel, and by turning the light of the Bible on the problems of the home-life and cultural life. Chairman: Mr. Hans Munck, principal of the folk-highschool, Skaade, Højbjerg. Secretary: Mr. Verner Kragskov, Århus. Staff: 1 paid employee, Budget: kr. 60.000. Funds collected: kr. 59.000. – There are in Denmark 600 circles and a high-school. International conventions are held, whereby the movement has spread to other countries, *e. g.* Finland, Norway, Sweden, and Holland.

De Danske Ungdomsforeninger (The Danish Youth Organizations)
Address: the office, Hjerting pr. Rødding. Founded in 1903.
Aim: To support the voluntary youth work in towns and in the country, to contribute to the strengthening of solidarity and fellowship among the young, to guide them towards the goal: a young generation of intelligent, Danish Christians. Chairman: The Rev. Helge Grell, minister of the Herning Valgmenighed. Secretary: Mr. Christian Christensen, of Hjerting pr. Rødding. Staff: 1 besides 4 consultants. Budget: kr. 105.000 annually. Finances: The National Organization obtains most of its funds from the subscriptions of members. – The National Organization publishes a weekly magazine, the "Dansk Ungdom" (Danish Youth).

Det Økumeniske Fællesråd i Danmark (Ecumenical Council of Denmark)
Address: 11, Nørregade, Copenhagen K. Founded in 1939.
Aim: *Det økumeniske Fællesråd i Danmark* maintains the contacts of the Danish National Church with other Danish denominations which have direct or indirect contacts with the World Council of Churches, with which *Det økumeniske Fællesråd* is affiliated. *Fællesrådet* works for mutual understanding among the denominations in Denmark, for a wider knowledge of the ecumenical work, and endeavours to strengthen the ties between the Scandinavian Churches. Chairman: The Right Reverend H. Fuglsang-Damgaard D.D. Secretary: The Rev. Henning Talman. Staff: 2. Budget: kr. 20.000. Funds collected kr. 16.000.

Credo (Student Evangelical Fellowship)
Work on a biblical basis among undergraduates and adolescents at schools.
Address: 115 A, Gothersgade, 3rd floor, Copenhagen K.
Founded 1956.

Purpose: Spreading the Gospel among undergraduates and adolescent school-pupils with a call to personal faith in Christ, to a strengthening the Christian community, and a life in the service of Jesus Christ as Our Lord and Savior. Staff: 1 – besides unpaid voluntary workers. Annual Budget: kr. 30.000–40.000. Funds collected: kr. 30.000.

Credo co-operates with similar movements in the other Scandinavian countries and keeps up connections with the International Fellowship of Evangelical Students (I.F.E.S.).

Danmarks Kristelige Gymnasiastbevægelse (Danish Christian High School Movement)
Address: 24, Amaliegade, Copenhagen K.
Founded in 1897.
Purpose: To bring to the pupils of our *gymnasiums* the message of Jesus Christ as preached by the Danish National Church, to present the problems of the Age in a Christian light, to provide the background for a free Christian fellowship.
Chairman: The Rev. Bertil Wiberg, Fårevejle. Secretary: Mr. Jørgen Henningsen. Total Staff: deputies among the pupils of the *gymnasiums:* 70. Voluntary undergraduate leaders of the movement's arrangements: 60.
Budget: kr. 50.000. Funds collected: kr. 20.000.

Danmarks Kristelige Studenterbevægelse (Student Christian Movement of Denmark)
Address: 23, Ny Østergade, Copenhagen K.
Founded 1892.
Aim: To bring to undergraduates the Christian message as preached in the Danish National Church, to work for the active participation

of the undergraduates in the Church's services and Mission, to participate in the Christian debate of cultural subjects, and to provide the undergraduates with a suitable background for undergraduate fellowship and recreational activities. Chairman: The Rev. S. C. Kemp. Secretary: Mr. Ole Andersen, B.D. There are local branches of Student Christian Movement of Denmark at the universities of Århus and Copenhagen.

In Copenhagen the International centre co-operates with the Student Movement for closer contacts between foreign students staying in this country for their studies and Danish undergraduates and Danish homes.

Dansk Kirke i Udlandet (The Danish Church Abroad)
Address: 10, Frederiksberggade, Copenhagen K.
Founded in 1910, on an Evangelical-Lutheran basis and in affiliation with the National Church.
Aim: To work for the preservation, revival, and growth of Faith with the organization of believers within a Christian Community of congregations, and wherever young Danes meet in Christian Youth organizations.

Besides active evangelization the Dansk Kirke i Udlandet aims to preserve among our countrymen abroad the love of our country, its language, and history. The Danish King and Queen are the D.K.U.'s Protectors. President: The Right Reverend, Bishop H. Fuglsang-Damgaard, D.D. Chairman: Mr. A. P. Christensen. Office manager: Mr. Johan Funck. Head of the Information Service in Denmark: The National Secretary Mr. G. Winter-Johannsen, Åbyhøj. Total Staff: in Denmark 2, besides office staff. Abroad 39 priests and 27 secretaries. Of these 25 priests and 9 secretaries are working in South Slesvig. Budget: kr. 2.896.000, of which kr. 1.524.000 is provided through a Government Grant. Funds collected: kr. 1.372.000. Besides the permanently appointed clergymen and secretaries, a number of priests are sent for short stays in Sweden, to conduct services and give lectures. Besides, Danes in South America are visited by a Danish clergyman located in Buenos Aires.

Dansk Sømandskirke i Fremmede Havne (The Danish Seamen's Church in Foreign Ports)
Address: 2, Bülowsvej, Copenhagen V. Founded in 1867.
Aim: To bring the message of the Church to sailors by sending out clergymen and other personel to the foreign ports most visited by Danish sailors, and also by other suitable means.
Chairman: The Right Reverend, Bishop Erik Jensen, Aalborg, General Secretary: The Rev. Ingstrup Mikkelsen. Secretaries for the Home Country: The Rev. Leif Lam and the Rev J. Højgaard Hansen. Staff: 15 sailors' priests, besides assistants, caretakers, and housewives. Budget: kr. 905.696. Funds collected: a Government Grant of kr. 464.174. The rest of the budget is financed through voluntary contributions. Besides in the various places where the missions are at work funds are collected which are not entered into the general accounts.

Den Danske Diakonissestiftelse (The Danish Deaconess Institution)
Address: 1, Peter Bangsvej, Copenhagen F. Founded in 1863.
Aim: On a National Church basis to train and send out nursing sisters to serve and perform works of charity and love among the sick, the destitute, and others suffering from spiritual or physical distress.
Chairman: Mr. H. Koldby Nielsen of the Ministry of Social Affairs. Principal: The Rev. Johannes W. Jacobsen. Staff: 300 nursing sisters and several hundred other personnel (doctors, nurses, and others). Budget: about kr. 15.000.000. Funds collected: kr. 243.692. To-day the nursing sisters are working as hospital nurses, visiting nurses, welfare-workers looking after children, the aged, and chronic invalids, and as parish-nurses.

Diakonissehuset Sankt Lukas Stiftelsen (The Deaconess-House Saint Luke Institution)
Address: 20, Bernstorffsvej, Hellerup. Founded in 1900.
Aim: To train and send out sisters to be the servants of the Church and do works of Christian Charity.
Chairman: Mr. H. W. Sprechler. Principals: Sister Eva Lyngby, and the Rev. Johannes Müller. Staff: 250 sisters and numerous other

employees (doctors, nurses, and others). Budget: kr. 7 or 8 millions. Funds collected: kr. 100.000–200.000 annually. The sisters of the Sankt Lukas Stiftelse constitute a community, sharing both their work, earnings, and Christian Life. The Sankt L. St. runs a hospital, a nursing home for babies, and an orphanage. The hospital runs a school for nurses with facilities for training children's nurses and matrons.

Evangelisk Alliance i Danmark (The Evangelical Alliance)
Address: 12, Skansebjerg, Brønshøj. Founded in 1885.
Aim: The *Evangelisk Alliance* is an ecumenical organization of most Evangelical Churches. The alliance endeavours to bring about a better understanding among Christians of different Faith. It invites to common prayers, studies of the Word of God, and discussions both of what separates, and what unites the Churches.
Chairman: The Rev. Aage Bjerno, Bellahøj Church, Copenhagen. Secretary: Mr. Poul Rasmussen, sacristan of Bellahøj Church. Staff: a committee of 4 members of the National Church and 7 Free Church members. Budget: kr. 15.000. Funds collected: circa 13.000 –14.000 annually.

Kolonien Filadelfia (The Philadelphia Colony)
Address: Dianalund. Founded in 1897.
Purpose: On Christian lines to provide hospital treatment of epileptics and others suffering from organic diseases of the nervous system, mental disorders, and nervousness in order to enable them once more to fill their place in the community, or, failing this, to provide for them a home, the needful care, etc.
Chairman: The former Minister of Ecclesiastical Affairs, Mr. Vilhelm Fibiger. Managers: Principal of the Nursing Sisters' House, Sister Eva Hoff. Principal of the Nursing Sisters' House and the Male Nurses' School, the Rev. Vilhelm Kolthoff Nielsen.
The K. F. is an endowed institution within the Evangelical-Lutheran Church, and at the same time an approved hospital for epileptics (about 780), mental patients (about 200), and a sanatorium for nervous patients. The Colony runs, among other facilities, a Nursing

Sisters' Home and a School for Male Nurses. There are about 660 staff, of whom 30 are nursing sisters, 110 male nurses and student male nurses. Budget: kr. 18.000.000 annually. Funds collected: kr. 25.000.

Landsforbundet Frivilligt Drenge-Forbund (Volunteer Boys' Organization)
Address: 6, Hjalmar Brantings Plads, Copenhagen Ø. Founded in 1902.
Aim: To do the work of the Kingdom of Christ among boys by bringing them under the influence of Christian men. Further, to carry on preventive, stimulating, and protective work among them by promoting mental and physical health, discipline, civility, punctuality, and other characteristics of true Christian manhood, and also training them in such sports as may be turned to practical use.
Chairman: The Rev. Poul Schou, Dean of Haderslev. Secretary: Secretary-General, Mr. Willy Gravesen. Total staff: 5 paid secretaries and about 4000 unpaid leaders all over the country. The National Association is made up op 355 local branches, affiliated with the parish church or the Y.M.C.A.
F.D.F. co-operates with The Boys' Brigade of Great Britain, the Ansgarsförbundet of Sweden, and The Poikien Keskus of Finland.

Landsforbundet Frivilligt Pige-Forbund (Volunteer Girls' Organization)
Address: 6, Hjalmar Brantings Plads, Copenhagen Ø. Founded in 1952.
Aim: In the spirit of the National Church to gather girls of all classes of the community in order, through the comradeship of the girls and the influence of grown-up women, to guide their development towards truly Christian lives.
Chairman: Mr. Willy Gravesen, Fredensborg. Secretaries: Mrs. Bodil Hansen and Miss Esther Pedersen. Staff: Executive, staff, district-workers, district-leaders, group-leaders, and instructors totalling 320. Budget: kr. 26.100. The *F.P.F.* is affiliated and co-operates with the parish churches throughout the country. Besides the F.P.F. works

in close co-operation with the F.D.F. the Ansgarsförbundet of Sweden, the Poikien Keskus of Finland, the Girls' Life of England, and Girls' Guildry of Scotland.

Det Københavnske Kirkefond (The Copenhagen Church Fund)
Address: 18, Aaboulevarden, Copenhagen N. Founded in 1896.
Aim: To make a contribution to a decent solution of problems arising from the lack of churches in Copenhagen and District, and so to support the National Church in its efforts to further the Kingdom of God and as a home for the life of the congregation.
Chairman: Mr. Hans Højsgaard, manager. Secretary: Secretary-General, the Rev. Cai Rasmussen. Staff: 8 paid assistants. Budget: kr. 600.000. Funds collected: The whole budget is paid for by voluntary contributions. – The *Kirkefondet* has been active in the building of many churches in Copenhagen and District.

Kirkelig Forening for Den Indre Mission i Danmark (The Church Association of Home Mission in Denmark)
Address: Indre Missions Hus, 21, Bernstorffsgade, Copenhagen V.
Aim: On an Evangelical-Lutheran basis and as far as possible in co-operation with the clergymen of the National Church to work for a revival of the faith and the union of the faithful in the community of the Saved.
Chairman: The Rev. Kr. Friis, parish priest of Farsø. National Secretary: Mr. Stefan Ottesen. Staff: 144 missionaries, 142 book colporteurs. Budget: kr. 2.383.796. Funds collected: 1.332.558. – The Society owns a publishing house, Lohses Forlag (manager: Mr. A. Lodberg), a printing house, Missionstrykkeriet, the Missions Hotel "Hebron", and publishes The *Indre Missions Tidende* and several other periodicals. Besides the Society owns 762 mission meeting houses all over the country.

Kirkemusikkredsen (The Church Music Circle)
Address: 147 A Bagsværdvej, Lyngby.
Founded 1950.

Aim: Through meetings, lectures, study-circles, concerts, and publications to work for the improvement of Danish church music.
Chairman: Ulrich Teuber M. A., organist.
Annual budget: about kr. 1.200 besides varying contributions from collections, etc.

Kirkens Korshær (The Church Army)
Address: Nikolaj Kirke, Copenhagen K.
Founded 1912.
Aim: *Kirkens Korshær* is part of the work of the Danish National Church. It works among the destitute. As far as possible the work is carried on in connection with local parish work.
Chairman: Mr. Vilhelm Asp Fenger, M.D. Secretary: The Rev. Ole Jensen. Staff: 110. Budget: kr. 3.275.000. Funds collected: kr. 1.325.737. – Besides the said 110 staff, about 1000 unpaid workers assist the work of the K.K. in various ways. Affiliated with the K.K. is the *St. Nicolay Tjenesten* (*vide* p. 159).

Kofoeds Skole (Kofoed's School)
Address: 34, Dronningensgade, Copenhagen K. Founded in 1928.
Aim: On Christian and democratic principles to succour and guide young men who have become social misfits, by helping them to help themselves in their efforts to regain a place in the community, thus working for the maintenance of self-respect, preservation of health, and training for life.
Chairman: Mr. Frantz Harlang. Principal: The Rev. Erhard Jørgensen. Staff: about 75. Budget: about kr. 1.5 millions. Funds collected: kr. 1.1 millions. – Through special departments the school endeavours to interest family members in their homes to help them to make homes for themselves, and fit them for the tasks and duties of the home. Besides the main school there is a school for young men and a home for youths.

Kristelig Forening for Unge Mænd og *Kristelig Forening for unge Kvinder* (The Y.M.C.A. and Y.W.C.A. in Denmark)
Address: 24, Amaliegade, Copenhagen K. Founded: The Y.M.C.A. in 1872, the Y.W.C.A. in 1883.

Aim: Preaching the Gospel as proclaimed in the Holy Bible and the doctrines of the Danish Evangelical Lutheran Church in order thereby to lead the young to the faith in Jesus Christ and to active participation in fellowship, witness, and service of the congregation, and to the life of intelligent, well-informed, and responsible Christians. Chairman of the Y.M.C.A.: the Rev. Ingv. Hovgaard, parish priest of Grønbæk; of the Y.W.C.A.: Mrs. Meta Hareskov. Secretary-General: The Rev. Aksel Nielsen. Staff: 70. Budget: kr. 1 million. Funds collected: kr. 830.000, and subscriptions kr. 283.000.

The Y.M.C.A. and Y.W.C.A. originate from the *Kirkelig Forening for Indre Mission* and are still working in close co-operation with this wing of the Church, while at the same time stressing that it is part of the National Church, and offering its assistance to all priests and parishes willing to accept it. The two movements share leadership and finances, the National Committees of the Y.M.C.A. and the Y.W.C.A. jointly making up their National Committee in Denmark.

K.F.U.M.-Spejderne i Danmark (Y.M.C.A.-Scouts in Denmark)
Address: 3, Vangehusvej, Copenhagen Ø. Founded in 1910.
Aim: Through wholesome, character-forming hobbies to train boys for useful, unselfish citizenship. Further, in co-operation with the National Church to carry on evangelization among its members.
Chairman: Mr. Tage Kampmann. Secretary of the corps: Mr. Elis Hansen. Staff: the staff of the central office numbers 10. Throughout the country there are about 2.400 voluntary adult leaders. Funds collected: Monthly membership subscriptions, grants from the *Frilufts-rådet* (Open Air Sports Council); occasional National Lotteries. The corps is affiliated with the Boy Scouts' International Bureau.

K.F.U.K.-Spejderne i Danmark (Y.W.C.A. Girl Guides in Denmark)
Address: 24, Amaliegade, Copenhagen K. Founded in 1919.
Aim: Through the efforts of Christian leaders to disseminate the Kingdom of God among children and adolescents. In obedience to the scout law and the international scout promise to carry on preventive and preservative work by occupying the girl guides with healthy and interesting hobbies in their spare time.

152

Chairman: Miss Esther Skjøt-Pedersen. Administrative Secretary: Miss Grethe Nedergaard. Staff: 3 secretaries, 3 clerks, 12 members of the Executive Committee and 1000 adult leaders.

Kristelig Lytter- og Fjernseerforening (The Danish Christian Radio and Television Audience Association)
Address: The Rev. S. A. Olsen, Vonsild. Founded 1926.
Aim: The association which is non-political and independent of Church movements aims to represent the members in their relations with the authorities, and to maintain the rights to which, by law, radio-listeners and television-viewers are entitled. The association will work for the best possible radio and television programmes – preferably of a Christian and cultural kind. – Chairman: The Rev. S. A. Olsen, parish priest of Vonsild. Budget: kr. 30.000. – The association, with its membership of 110.000, is the country's largest organization of radio-listeners and television-viewers. At the moment it has an elected representative on the Radio Council and the Programme Selection Committee. Besides, the association lends wireless sets to the poor, the sick, and to invalids, and grants travelling bursaries to employees of The Danish State Radio.

Kristeligt Dagblad (The Daily Christian News)
Address: 5, Frederiksborggade, Copenhagen K. Founded in 1896.
Aim: To publish a daily newspaper based on the lines of the National Church.
Chairman: The Rev. H. P. Honoré, rural dean of Vejlby, Editor-in-chief: Mr. Bent A. Koch. Staff: 123. Budget: kr. 4,8 millions.

Det Lutherske Verdensforbunds Danske Nationalkomité (The Danish National Committee of the Lutheran World Federation)
Address: 11, Nørregade, Copenhagen K. Founded in 1954.
Aim: To maintain the contacts of the Danish National Church with other Lutheran Churches – among others with *The Lutheran World Federation*.
Chairman: The Right Reverend, Bishop H. Høgsbro. Secretary: The Rev. Mr. Henning Talman. Staff: 1.

Den Kristne Lægmandsbevægelse (L.Y.M.) (The Christian Layman Society)
Address: 105, Kongensgade, Fredericia. Founded 1912.
Aim: To lead men to Christ, to strengthen Christian brotherhood, and inspire men to accept their responsibility for Christ's command for the missions at home and abroad.
Chairman: Mr. Kaj V. Mollerup, headmaster, Odense. Secretary: Mr. C. V. Garm, Fredericia. Annual budget: kr. 100.000 (including funds granted to various foreign mission societies). The society is supported by 2.500 regular contributors. There is no permanent membership, but all men can attend meetings and other arrangements.

Den Danske Folkekirkes Mellemkirkelige Råd (Church of Denmark Council on Inter-Church Relations)
Address: 11, Nørregade, Copenhagen K. Founded in 1954.
Aim: To keep up the contacts of the Danish National Church with foreign Churches – f. inst. through the official contact with World Council of Churches and Lutheran World Federation.
Chairman: The Right Reverend W. Westergaard Madsen, Bishop of Copenhagen. Secretary: The Rev. Henning Talman. Staff: 2. Budget: kr. 25.000. Funds collected: kr. 15.000. The secretariat of the *Mellemkirkelige Råd* provides information to foreigners about Danish church-life and visits to ecclesiastical institutions.

Dansk Missionsråd (The Danish Mission Council)
Address: 11, Nørregade, Copenhagen K. Founded in 1912.
Aim: To be an organ for the co-operation of the various branches of the Danish Foreign Mission with foreign and international mission societies, to represent before Danish and foreign authorities such common interests as the Danish Foreign Missions may have, to work for the awakening and dissemination throughout Denmark of the love and understanding of the World Missions, to collect and distribute gifts to the Foreign Missions, and in Denmark to co-operate with the ecumenical bodies.
Chairman: The Right Reverend H. Høgsbro, Nykøbing F. Staff: 3. Budget: about kr. 500.000. Funds collected: kr. 500.000.

Associated Council of the World Council Churches' Division of World Mission and Evangelism. Maintains relations with the Lutheran World Federation, Department of World Missions on behalf of the Danish Lutheran Mission Societies.

The Mission Council is an organ for the co-operation of 14 National Church Mission Societies and 3 Free Church Mission Societies (Baptists, Methodists, and Salvation Army). The following Mission Societies are members of the Danish Mission Council.

Brødremenighedens Danske Mission (Moravian Mission, Denmark)
Address: Christiansfeld. Founded in 1843.
Aim: Mission. Chairman: The Rev. K. Robert Hansen, principal, Fårevejle. Secretary: Bishop Elmo Knudsen, Christiansfeld. Staff: 36. Budget: kr. 565.000. The Moravian Brethren's Mission is a branch of the Herrnhuter Brüdergemeinde.

Den Nordiske Kristne Buddhistmission (Scandinavian Christian Mission to Buddhists)
Address: Svinget 12, V., Copenhagen S. Founded in 1922.
Aim: To carry the Gospel of Jesus Christ to the Buddhists of East Asia. Chairman of the Scandinavian Executive Committee: Missions director C. G. Diehl, Ph. D. For Denmark: The Rev. Niels Nøjgaard, D.D. Administrative director: Mr. Vilh. Schröder. Staff in the missions-fields: 3 Danish married couples, 1 Norwegian woman missionary, 10 Chinese and 2 Japanese paid assistants. Budget: kr. 850.000, of which kr. 250.000 in Denmark. Funds collected in Denmark: kr. 207.000. – The Scandinavian Christian Buddhist Mission is an Inter-Scandinavian Mission with local administrations in Denmark, Norway, and Sweden. Mission in Hong Kong based on the Tao Fong Shan Institute, and in Kyoto and the Misawa Valley in Japan. In the last-mentioned district was built (in 1963) "Shin Rei San", a Brethren's Home for religious seekers, affiliated with an agricultural school for the training of young Japanese.

Det Danske Missionsselskab (Danish Mission Society)
Address: 24, Strandagervej, Hellerup. Founded in 1821.

Aim: The Danske Missionsselskab is based on the doctrines of the Danish Evangelical Lutheran National Church. Its aim is to carry on evangelization among Moslems and other non-Christians, and to help new Churches to become independent and to start missions. Chairman: The Rev. C. Rendtorff. Secretaries: Secretary-General, The Rev. E. W. Nielsen (the work in Foreign missions fields), and Secretary-General, Mr. Erik Petersen (the work in Denmark). Staff: 84 missionaries in Africa and Asia, 14 secretaries employed by the Executive for public relations work in Denmark. Budget: kr. 3.3 millions. Funds collected: sufficient to cover the budget. – The Danish Mission Society co-operates with Churches in Tanganyika, Aden, India (State of Madras and Orissa), Taiwan, and Japan. The mission is carried out in co-operation with these Churches.

Den Danske Ethiopier Mission (Danish Ethiopian Mission)
Address: 96, Østersøgade, Copenhagen Ø. Founded in 1948.
Aim: To carry the Gospel to Ethiopia by a mission engaged in evangelization, medicine, and education. Chairman: medical superintendent, Mr. Niels Harhoff, M.D., Skanderborg. Secretary: P. Mengel-Christensen. Staff: 2 teachers, and 3 nurses. Budget: kr. 166.423. Funds collected: kr. 20.000. The Ethiopian Mission works in a district about 450 kilometres south of Addis Abeba, Capital of Ethiopia.

Den Danske Israelmission (The Danish Mission to the Jews)
Address: 5, Lipkesgade, Copenhagen Ø. Founded in 1885.
Aim: To establish contacts between Israel and the Church, to preach the Gospel of Jesus as the Messiah of Israel, to combat anti-Semitism, to give the congregation information of Israel, to awaken and foster its love of the Jewish people. Chairman: The Rev. Axel Torm. Staff: 7. Budget: kr. 318.560. Funds collected: kr. 260.000. This Mission is active in Jaffa, Israel, Paris, Algiers, and Copenhagen.
In Jaffa the Mission co-operates with the Tabeetha School of the Scottish Church Mission.

156

Kherwara-Missionen (The Kherwara-Mission)
Address: 28, B, 7th floor, Bellahøj, Brønshøj. Founded 1944.
Aim: To carry on Mission work among the Bhil people and other nations living among them in North West India and Pakistan.
Chairman: The Rev. A. V. Holm, parish priest of Havreholm. Secretary: Mr. Harry Pedersen. Staff: 1 missionary and 5 Indian assistants. Budget: kr. 60.000.

Kvindelige Missions Arbejdere (Women Missionary Workers)
Address: 3, Mynstersvej (3rd floor), Copenhagen V. Founded in 1900.
Aim: Works among Armenians in Libanon and among the Bhil people of India.
Chairman: Mrs. Elsa Vind, Sanderumgaard, Fraugde, Island of Funen. Secretary: Miss Alma Hvalsø Petersen. Treasurer: Miss Else Marie Clausen. Staff: in Libanon, 2 missionaries, in India 2 missionaries. Budget: kr. 360.000. Funds collected: kr. 443.687.

Luthersk Missionsforening (Danish Lutheran Mission)
Address: 93, Nansensgade, Copenhagen K. Founded in 1868.
Aim: Evangelization at home and abroad. Chairman: Mr. Aage Jensen, Gram. Secretary: Miss Juta Rasmussen. Staff in Denmark and the mission fields: 80. Budget: kr. 600.000. Funds collected: kr. 525.000. – *Luthersk Missionsforening* belongs to the National Church. It runs a number of schools in Denmark. Danish missionaries sent out by the *Luthersk Missionsforening* are at work in Tanganyika and in Suriname in South America.

Dansk Pathanmission (Danish Pathan Mission)
Address: 33, Overgaden neden Vandet, Copenhagen K.
Founded in 1903.
Aim: Danish Pathan Mission is the name of a mission activity based on the Evangelical Lutheran Church in Denmark, whose aim is to bring the Gospel to the people of Afghanistan. Afghanistan being closed to the Christian Mission, The Danish Pathan Mission temporarily works in a mission-field which has been given it in the north

west border province of Pakistan. Chairman: Professor Torben Christensen, D.D. Secretary: The Rev. G. Borg-Hansen. Staff: 2 Danish missionaires, 2 Pakistan priests. Budget: kr. 150.000. Funds collected: kr. 112.641. – At the moment the Danish Pathan Mission is active in Peshawar and Malakand in North-West Pakistan.

Dansk Santal Mission (The Danish Santal Mission)
Address: 11, Nørregade, Copenhagen K. Founded 1867.
Aim: A Foreign Mission Society. Its field in India includes the states of Bihar, West Bengal, Malda, and Assam, besides, after the secession of Pakistan from India, East Pakistan. Chairman: The Rev. Axel Thorman, Randers. Secretary: Secretary-General Miss Edith Bender. Staff: 20 missionaries, 1 secretary-general, 3 travelling secretaries, and office personnel. Budget: kr. 800.000. Funds collected: kr. 773.000. The work in India and Pakistan is carried out in co-operation with Norwegians and Americans (37 Norwegian and 16 American Missionaries). In 1950 the Santal Church was given its own constitution, and since 1958 the Bishop of this Church has been an Indian, the Right Reverend Munshi Tudu. In the Mission field are 4 hospitals, 2 leper colonies, 5 colleges, 107 elementary and secondary schools, 12 poli-clinics, 1 nurses' training school, a theological seminary, and several other institutions, all run by the Mission. 500 groups throughout the country back its activity and collect funds for the work.

Dansk Forenet Sudan Mission (Danish Sudan Mission)
Address: 11, Frodesgade, Århus C. Founded in 1911.
Aim: In co-operation with The Lutheran Church of Christ in the Sudan, Nigeria to preach the Gospel of Jesus Christ. Secretaries: Secretary-General Mr. I. Engskov, National-Secretary Mr. A. Pilgaard Pedersen. Staff: 72 missionaries in Nigeria, West Africa, 11 ful-time paid employees in Denmark. Budget: kr: 1.721.000. Funds collected: kr. 1.527.000.

Østerlandsmissionen (Danish Mission to the Orient)
Address: 115 A, Gothersgade, København K. Founded in 1898.

158

Aim: To reach the Moslems by preaching the Gospel and by co-operation with the local Christian Churches – where such Churches exist. Chairman: The Rev. Villy Sørensen, parish priest of Kerteminde. Secretary: Miss Ebba Nikolajsen, Århus C. Staff: 9 missionaries besides two who are being trained. Budget: kr. 360.000. The entire budget is paid by means of collected funds.

Den Danske Folkekirkes Nødhjælp (Church of Denmark Inter-Church Aid Committee)
Address: 11, Nørregade, Copenhagen K. Founded in 1922.
Aim: To give financial and other support to destitute Churches and Church activities – usually outside Denmark. Funds are obtained through current public collections and collections in the churches. Chairman: The Rev. Immanuel Felter, Dean of Maribo. Secretary: The Rev. Viggo Mollerup. Staff: 3. Budget: kr. 800.000. Funds collected: kr. 660.000. Besides financial aid the Committee gives material aid especially by distributing second-hand clothes and milk powder. The average annual value of this aid in goods is about kr. 700.000. The *D.D.F.N.* is the Danish branch of the ecumenical charity work. It works in close co-operation with the Relief Departments of the Lutheran World Federation, represents these institutions in their relations with the Church of Denmark. Structurally the D.D.F.N. is a branch of the Church of Denmark Council on Inter-Church Relations, and the members of the Executive are all members of the National Church.

St. Nicolai Tjenesten (The St. Nicolai Service)
Address: St. Nicolai Church, Copenhagen K. Founded in 1957.
Aim: The St. Nicolai Service is a Church service aiming to take personal care of persons desiring a talk about their problems. Chairman: The Right Reverend, Bishop Fuglsang-Damgaard. Secretary: The Rev. Ole Jensen. Staff: 90—100 clergymen besides about 200 assistants. Budget: the administration of the St. Nicolai Service is in the hands of the *Kirkens Korshær* (*vide* p. 151). – The houses of the St. Nicolai Service are open from 9 p.m. to 3 a.m.; on Sundays and holidays from 1 p.m. to 3 a.m. Affiliated with centre inter-

national d'information des services de secours par téléphone, 20, Promenade St. Antoine, Genève (Suisse).

Samfundet Dansk Kirkesang (The Society for Danish Church Singing)
Address: 14 Fogedmarken, Copenhagen N.
Founded 1927.
Aim: The continuation of the pioneer work for the improvement of hymn-singing within the Danish Church started by the composer Thomas Laub. The Society works partly through its publications and partly through annual national meetings for the dissemination of knowledge of *hymn-tunes* and of the manifold problems of liturgical music.
Chairman: Henrik Glahn Ph.D.; secretary: Torben Schouboe, organist.

De Samvirkende Menighedsplejer (The Copenhagen Association of Parochial Social Services)
Address: 28, Vendersgade, Copenhagen K. Founded 1902.
Aim: To work for the closer co-operation of parish charities in Copenhagen and District, assist them financially and in other ways in carrying out work of the parish charities among the distressed inhabitants of the parishes. Chairman: Mr. Kurt Elmvang. Secretary: Secretary-General, the Rev. Immanuel Hansen. Staff: 20 working at the Central Office and a good 1000 voluntary workers in the parishes. Budget: kr. 3.711.312. Capital: kr. 6.728.190. Funds collected: kr. 450.000.

Kristeligt Studenter-Settlement (Christian Students' Settlement)
Address: Saxogade 91, Copenhagen V. Founded 1911.
Aim: On Christian principles to make an effort to alleviate the social, pedagogical, and mental evils of a poor residential quarter of the Capital, to arrange meetings of the working-classes with undergraduates and professional people in order thereby to create a better understanding of social problems, and through its work to increase the feeling of social responsibility in all classes of the community. Chairman: Professor Svend Holm-Nielsen, D.D. Secretary: The principal

Mr. Otto Krabbe. Staff: 10 employees, besides about 75 voluntary workers – most of them young undergraduates. Budget: kr. 370.000. Funds collected: kr. 120.000. – The Students' Settlement is an endowed institution including about 65 groups of children, adolescents, adults, and aged persons meeting for weekly gatherings: recreation centres, study circles, and courses. Guidance office, recreation centres for school-children, and summer camps. The Settlement is approved by the public authorities for its preventive work for children and adolescents and receives a public grant of kr. 179.000.

CONTENTS

THE DANISH CHURCH

Editor

Poul Hartling

Translation

Sigurd Mammen

Cover

Faarevejle Church, Sealand,
an Inga Aistrup photo.

Plates

Skandinavisk Reproduktion, Copenhagen

Printing

J. Jørgensen & Co, Copenhagen

Acknowledgements

For assistance in making this book the Danish Institute expresses its gratitude to dr. *Erik Dal,* the Royal Library, for valuable information, to the publishers *De Unges Forlag* for permission to use illustrations from the book *Kirken den er et gammelt Hus,* by *Tage Christiansen,* and to the publishers *Gyldendal* and the *National Museum* for rare church illustrations.

Copyright

Det danske Selskab
1964

Printed in Denmark

Sk. Mary's of Sæby, North Jutland. All the streets of this little town seem
centered upon the 15th century church tower.

The Church of Our Lady of Kalundborg. Tradition has it that, about 1170, the headman Esbern Snare had the church built on a hill surrounded by a wall close to his castle in the Upper Town. By its strange architecture this church, one of the most peculiar in Scandinavia, as well as one of our very oldest brick churches, reminds of a castle rather than of a church, and theories have been advanced to the effect that it has had fortifications. It seems more probable, however, that its unusual plan is a Scandinavian adaptation of the Byzantine domed church. The ground plan is the equal-armed Greek cross.

On Denmark's one rocky island the circular churches are uniquely represented. In the rest of Denmark similar churches are only preserved in Thorsager in Jutland, Horne in the island of Funen, and Bjernede in Zealand. Bornholm has several, of which that of Østerlars is one of the most impressive. The circular churches were built not only as churches, but also as fortresses. So they have several storeys, designed both for the protection and defence of the population, which, in the event of enemy inroads on the coast retreated to their churches. Østerlars Church, Island of Bornholm. 12th century. The shingled roof is probably 17th century. This is the largest of the island's four circular churches.

The Rococo reredos of *Vor Frelsers Kirke* (Our Saviour's Church) in Copenhagen.

Bottom of next page : Frederik's Church, Copenhagen, com
monly known as *Marmorkirken* (The Marble Church), co
secrated in 1894. Architect F. Meldahl.

The tower of Our Saviour's Church, Copenhagen, with Laur. de Thurah's copper-covered spiral spire, which was added to the church in 1747-1752.

St. Nicolaj's, Copenhagen. Built in the 13th century, destroyed by fire in 1795, rebuilt in the opening years of this century. Today the domicile of the Church Army and, besides, of the Naval Museum.

The Cathedral of Our Lady in Copenhagen is the oldest church in the Capital in which divine services are still held. It owes its present form to the architect C. F. Hansen. He rebuilt the church in the years 1811-1829, after it had been destroyed by the English Bombardment of Copenhagen in 1807. The picture shows the tower and portal of the Cathedral in the narrow street.

Next page.
With its tall slender towers Roskilde Cathedral dominates the entire town. It is built of red brick on a foundation of granite. It takes the form of a Latin Cross, whose arms, however, no longer protrude from the walls of the aisles.

The Grundtvig Church, Copenhagen, built 1921-1940. Architect P.V. Jensen Klint. Our picture gives a front view of the tower, plainly showing the architect's intention to create a cathedral in the style of the Danish village church with late Gothic corbie gables and vertical lines. In order also to pay homage to Grundtvig as our greatest hymn writer, it was made to remind of the front of a gigantic organ. The building of this vast church - this century's largest in Denmark—was paid for through collections all over the country, contributions coming in from wide circles of the Danish people.